MW01008785

# FIVE THOUSAND YEARS OF CHINESE NATION

Zhang Yantu

 **FOREIGN LANGUAGES PRESS**

First Edition 2007
Fourth Printing 2011

ISBN 978-7-119-04636-5
© Foreign Languages Press, Beijing, 2007

*Published by*
Foreign Languages Press
   24 Baiwanzhuang Road, Beijing 100037, China
   Home Page: http: //www.flp.com.cn
*Distributed by*
China International Book Trading Corporation
   35 Chegongzhuang Xilu, Beijing 100044, China
   P.O.Box 399, Beijing, China

*Printed in the People's Republic of China*

# PREFACE

China, an age-old nation with a history of nearly five thousand years, has a time-honored splendid civilization like many other nations in the world.

Do you want to open the gate to the treasures of such a giant nation with a long-standing history and civilization? Do you desire a magic wand to lead you easily through the long historical corridor of this great Eastern nation and see the brilliance of its history?

Then, please open this book. It is a magic wand that helps you understand Chinese history with ease, as well as a window providing a convenient view on China.

This book tells nearly 100 well-known stories from remote antiquity to the Revolution of 1911 in time sequence and takes key historical events and figures as the main line. In compiling the book, we have striven to present the social changes, wars and battles, science and technology, and culture and art during China's five thousand years of history in a series of accurate, vivid and concise stories. The book is a historical documentary with varied extraordinary splendor rather than a heavy, dull academic work.

The book vividly portrays a good number of historical figures, including feudal emperors of supremacy, wise and thundering generals and commanders, upright, loyal and virtuous people, merciless officials and treacherous ministers, righteous, dauntless and unbending national heroes and people of exceptional ability, and scrupulous and practical-minded scientists and thinkers of great learning and wisdom.

In the process of editing, we pursued faithfulness to historical facts, yet we avoided dry historical data. We placed emphasis on the readability of the text and illustrated the text with quite a few exquisite and vivid paintings, composing an interesting book excellent both in pictures and language. We hope that the book could lead you to appreciate the splendor of Chinese history and bring you the joy of reading at the same time.

# Contents

# PANGU CREATES HEAVEN AND EARTH

《 Bust reproduction of the Upper Cave Man, an ape man living in caves in Longgushan Mountain, Zhoukoudian, Beijing, c. 18,000 years ago.

What is the origin of the universe? How did the sun, the moon and the stars come into being? Who created the rivers, mountains and lands? How was mankind originated? Human beings have been pondering such questions from the earliest days. Our ancient ancestors tended to give answers through mythical tales. What was the traditional Chinese explanation for the beginning of the universe? Among the many creation myths found in China, the one featuring Pangu is the most widely known.

≫ Pangu, the creator of the heavens and earth.

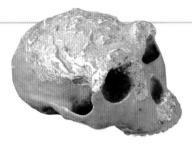

Bust reconstruction of Lantian Man; c. 1.15 million to 650,000 years ago, Lantian Man, a subspecies of *Homo erectus*, populated the area of Gongwangling, now part of Lantian County, Shaanxi Province.

The drawing illustrates the Tibetan concept of how human beings originated: a monkey gradually transforms into a human being after taking instruction from the Buddha.

Legend has it that in remote antiquity when the universe was yet to take shape, everything was chaos. The universe was like an egg, carrying Pangu, the first ancestor of humankind, exactly in the center of its yolk. Nurtured in this round hollow for 18,000 years, finally he picked up a handmade huge ax and wielded it with all his might to crack open the egg. The light, clear part of it floated up and formed the heavens, while the heavy, turbid matter stayed below to form earth. Pangu began to grow at a rate of three meters per day, and soon became a formidable giant.

Pangu was the only human being living in the universe he had just created. When he was happy, the sun shone; but when he was angry, black clouds gathered in the skies. When he cried, his tears turned into pouring rain. When he sighed, air puffed from his mouth to become gusts of wind.

At last, the giant died, sprawled out on the ground with his head to the east and feet to the west. His head transformed into Mt. Tai in today's Shandong Province, his feet into Mt. Huashan in today's Shaanxi Province, his stomach into Mt. Songshan in Henan Province, his left arm into Mt. Hengshan in Hunan Province, and his right arm into Mt. Hengshan in Shanxi Province, the five most famous mountains in China. His hair turned into trees, flowers and grasses covering the different lands.

Although nobody still believes this myth today, the Pangu story is firmly fixed in Chinese tradition. There is even an idiom relating to it: "Since Pangu created the heavens and earth," which means "for a very long time." This is perhaps because it symbolized the human aspiration to triumph over nature, and our most fertile creativity.

This reconstruction shows Peking Man carrying a deer. Peking Man, a subspecies of *Homo erectus*, lived 700,000 to 230,000 years ago; after acquiring the use of fire, these hominids no longer ate raw animal meat.

# NÜWA REPAIRS THE HEAVENS

A silk painting of Fuxi and Nüwa, dating back to the Tang Dynasty. The two ancestors of humankind are depicted as snakes with human heads. The upper parts of their bodies are embracing, while the lower parts are intertwined.

After the death of Pangu, the universe became empty of any human presence. It was not until many, many years later that Nüwa, another ancestor of humankind, appeared. She felt so lonely, she wanted to create more people to live with her.

One day, she began to make human figures, both male and female, out of yellow clay. Strangely, each came to life as soon as she blew her breath upon them. At last, all the figures she created acquired life, forming lively company gathered around her. As they lived and worked together, the adults gave birth to children. The playful infants grew up happy and carefree, then married and had their own children.

Unfortunately, while the human beings were living peacefully on earth, the universe was suffering serious damage. The ancient Chinese believed the heavens to be round, while the earth was square; at each corner of the square earth stood a pillar that propped up the heavens. With the passage of time, the pillars had decayed. As a result, the heavens began to shake violently as if about to collapse.

Major disaster then befell humankind. Many holes appeared in the sky, through which torrential rains poured down. Some regions of the earth caught fire, while others were flooded. Ferocious wild animals exploited the disorder to prey on humans. Cruel birds dove from the sky, seizing vulnerable people with their sharp talons. Human beings were thus plunged deeply into a perilous world.

At this critical juncture Nüwa came to their rescue. She mended the holes in the sky with red,

Painted ceramic pot, 5,000-6,000 years ago.

⚊ Nüwa repairing the heavens.

yellow, blue, white and black stones that she had melted over reed fires. Then she replaced the four decayed columns with the legs of an enormous tortoise she had caught. She also killed the black dragon that had caused the torrential rain. Owing to Nüwa's efforts, everything returned to normal, with the heavens repaired, the four supporting pillars were strengthened, the dangerous wild beasts and birds wiped out, the lands once again covered with vegetation, so that human beings were able to resume their peaceful life. Nüwa, the great goddess, had not only created human beings but also saved them from severe calamity.

⚊ Jade dragon, 5,000-6,000 years ago.

# EMPERORS HUANGDI AND YANDI

△ Emperor Huangdi.

Huangdi, or the Yellow Emperor, was one of the Five Emperors in prehistoric China, together with Zhuanxu, Diku, Yao and Shun, prominent tribe leaders of the patriarchal society. With the family name of Gongsun, and given name Xuanyuan, Huangdi was born a talented child. When he grew up, he was elected chief of his tribe, because of his readiness to help his fellow tribesmen. Later, he defeated and annexed a tribe led by Yandi, surnamed Jiang, in an armed conflict. After the takeover, Huangdi became the chief of the new tribe, with Yandi serving as his deputy. The Yan-Huang tribe is believed to be the embryo of the Chinese nation. The Chinese often refer to them-

⌄ Huangdi battling against Chiyou.

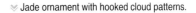

Red pottery vase in shape of human head.

selves as "descendants of Huandi and Yandi."

After the merger of the tribes of Yandi and Huangdi, the Jiuli tribe in the south began to move northeastward, threatening the Yan-Huang tribe. As he once had defeated Yandi in a battle, Chiyou, the arrogant chief of the Jiuli tribe, presumed the Yan-Huang tribe to be no match to him.

Chiyou was said to be a powerful figure. He had 81 brothers, all of whom were animals with human heads, each with eight arms and nine toes. Their foreheads were as strong as iron. Wearing colorful designs on their faces, these ferocious creatures could eat sand and stone. In order to cope with the threat from the Jiuli tribe, Yandi and Huangdi had many stone knives and axes carved, and a formidable force trained. At the same time, they devised a scrupulous defense plan.

A fierce battle between the two tribes finally broke out in Zhuolu. At the beginning, Huangdi ordered General Yinglong to block rivers and used the water to drown Chiyou's troops. Chiyou remained unfazed as he had the support of the gods of wind and rain, who sent strong winds and heavy rains. In response, Huangdi sent for Goddess Hanbo, who dispelled the winds and rains with scorching sunshine and dry gusts.

Beaten in the first round, Chiyou was forced to make the most of his powers. Using wizardry, he caused a heavy fog. In the blinding fog, which lasted for three days and nights, the warriors of the Yan-Huang tribe lost all sense of direction, unable to spot their enemies, and they struggled to stay together. Huangdi then ordered General Fenghou to construct a compass chariot to give directions. With the chariot, they found the location of Chiyou's headquarters.

When they launched the decisive attack, the complacent Chiyou was indulging in merrymaking, assuming a guaranteed victory in this battle. The offensive took him by complete surprise. He was beaten to the ground and taken prisoner before he had time to organize any significant counterattack. After their triumph, Yandi and Huangdi merged the Jiuli tribe into the Yan-Huang tribe.

Jade ornament with hooked cloud patterns.

# YAO PASSES THE THRONE TO SHUN

Yao.

Shun.

Yao and Shun were two of the Five Emperors in prehistoric China. Yao, surnamed Yinqi and styled Fangxun, was also known as Tang Yao because his fief was in a region called Tang.

Yao won popular support for his superb moral standards and high prestige. A prudent and respectable man, he had been able to strengthen the solidarity of different clans and tribes. Yao also gained respect for his simple way of living.

After 70 years on the throne, the 86-year-old tribal leader felt it time to pass his responsibilities onto a younger person. So he ordered announcements posted across the country, calling on people to recommend able candidates. Shortly after, people unanimously recommended Shun to succeed the old emperor.

Shun lived with his blind father and stepmother, who later gave birth to a son called Xiang. Xiang was lazy and arrogant. However, the father was always partial to him. Despite this, Shun was filial to his parents and kind to his half-brother. Having been told what kind of person Shun was, Yao decided to put him to a test, in order to see if he was qualified enough to be his successor. He married his two daughters Ehuang and Nüying to him, and sent him to work in different parts of the country.

Shun was first sent to farm at the foot of Lishan Mountain, where disputes often rose among the residents over the use of land. As soon as Shun arrived, they stopped quarrelling to focus on their farm work. Shun was also sent to fish among the fishermen. Before this, the fishermen were constantly embroiled in bloody squabbles over houses. However, immediately after Shun arrived, they shed their selfishness and befriended with each other. Wherever

Shun went, local people followed his leadership.

Delighted by the fine work that Shun had done, Yao presented him with a new gown, a zither and many sheep and cattle, in addition to building a barn for him. Shun's father and brother were so jealous that they plotted to kill him. One day, the father asked Shun to repair the roof of the barn, attempting to burn him to death by lighting a fire inside. The scheme was detected by Shun's two wives Ehuang and Nüying, who told him to take two large bamboo hats with him. When he saw the fire below, Shun jumped off the roof safely with a hat in each hand, like a pair of wings.

Although their first attempt was thus foiled, his father and Xiang did not give up. Several days later, his father told Shun to dig a well with the intention of burying him alive. However, Shun climbed out from under the dirt through an inclined channel he had dug. Xiang was playing a zither on a mat in Shun's house, when Shun showed up. Believing Shun had died, Xiang was shocked to the core.

"I was just thinking of you, my brother," exclaimed the hypocrite, "What took you so long to dig a well? I've been missing you to death."

Instead of scolding his cruel-hearted half-brother, Shun said, "You are so concerned about me, my dear brother. You are my dearest brother indeed."

Impressed by Shun's tolerance, Yao trusted him even more and handed over administrative power to him. In the twenty years that followed, Shun governed the country well, winning the widespread respect of the public. When he was over a hundred years old, Yao decided to retire. After taking an inspection tour throughout the country, he finally installed Shun as chief of the tribal alliance.

《 Yao passing the throne to Shun. After growing old, Yao decided to abdicate and pass on rule to Shun, a successor he selected through a series of tests. He also married his two beautiful daughters to Shun to assist him.

# DA YU CONQUERS THE FLOODS

⌃ Da Yu.

Legend has it that severe floods hit China during the reign of Yao, destroying houses, ravaging farmlands, and drowning tens of thousands of people. In order to save the country from calamity, Yao called on the public to recommend capable persons to deal with the floods. A man named Gun was recommended. For the ensuing nine years, he fought against the floods by building dams. While dams were constructed in one place, those in another place were destroyed. As a result, all his efforts came to nothing in the end. Yao sent Shun to inspect Gun's work. Seeing that Gun could do nothing to stop the floods, Shun had him executed and ordered his son Yu to continue the mission.

Yu took over the task. Learning from his father's failure, he decided to first conduct onsite research. Yu, together with his many aides including Yi and Houji, traveled extensively in the flood-stricken areas. They studied the topography of these areas, marking their findings with wooden logs. Based on their research, they came up with plans to tackle the floods.

As chief of the campaign against the floods, Yu set a good example for others. Everybody was moved to tears when they saw his blistered hands and feet. His calves and feet had been soaked in water for so long, that the nails of his toes and hair on his legs had all vanished. In the 13 years he was in charge of combating floods, he passed his home three times during his travels, but never once visited his home.

Yu found the correct approach to control the floods: by creating channels in the mountains, and by diverting the waters through those channels to big rivers and then to the sea. In Yu's time, a range of high mountains (between today's Hejin, Shanxi Province, and Hancheng, Shaanxi Province) blocked the surging Yellow River. Consequently, the

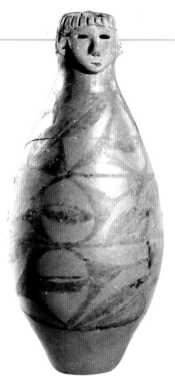

river breached its embankments, flooding the regions nearby.

Yu believed that this was the crux of the anti-flood campaign. He decided to create a gap in the mountain so that the river could continue its journey. After strenuous efforts, a gap was excavated. Now, the Yellow River could flow down through the gap. To commemorate this hero, people named the mountain "Longmen" (Dragon's Gate) Mountain, and the gap, "Yumenkou" (Gate of Yu). Yu was also extolled as "Da Yu" (Great Yu) for his remarkable contributions.

≪ Painted pottery vase.

⌄ Da Yu taming the floods.

# THE FALL OF THE XIA DYNASTY

Shang Tang.

When he died, Da Yu passed the throne to his son Qi, who founded the first slave dynasty in Chinese history, the Xia Dynasty, at the end of the 22nd and beginning of the 21st century BC. Dynastic rulers governed the country for over 400 years until 16th century BC, when Jie, an infamous tyrant, was overthrown.

At that time, the Shang, a tribe living along the lower reaches of the Yellow River who specialized in animal herding, rose rapidly. By the end of the Xia Dynasty, they had become a powerful tribe led by Tang, also known as Shang Tang or Cheng Tang.

Indignant over its corruption, Tang was determined to topple the Xia Dynasty. While acting ostensibly obedient to Jie, he secretly enhanced his own power. In order to facilitate military operations, he moved his tribe to Bo (today's Shangqiu, Henan Province). From Bo to the capital of the Xia Dynasty stretched a vast plain without any mountains or rivers, a geological advantage making it easy for large troops to maneuver. In Bo, Tang with his tolerance won the support of all his tribesmen. He also tried to boost his profile across the country, and to seek the approval of other tribes.

At that time, all tribal leaders believed in gods, and considered the worshipping of the heavens, the

Restored picture of a palace of the Xia Dynasty.

earth and their ancestors, to be of paramount importance. However, a tribe called Ge, not far from the Shang tribe, did not offer sacrifices at the correct time. Worse still, the people there themselves ate the cattle and sheep Tang had offered them for sacrificial use. They even went as far as to kill the young man who had brought the food sent by Tang to farmhands hired by some Ge nobles, and stole the food. This triggered a battle between the two tribes, in which the Ge was defeated. Tang took this opportunity to seize

⌃ Simuxin Bronze Vessel, used at sacrificial ceremony.

a number of nearby tribes. Tang's power gradually strengthened with these moves. However, the insensible, decadent Jie did not take note of Tang's ambitions.

Tang thought the time was ripe for overthrowing the Xia Dynasty, since many tribes, no longer able to bear the cruelty of the Xia, had seceded from the dynasty. Tang decided to launch a massive attack. He first imbued the soldiers with a desire to topple the Xia Dynasty by appealing to the aspirations of the heavens. As a result, all the soldiers fought heroically. At a decisive battle in Mingdi, Jie's troops suffered a major defeat. Jie fled to Nanchao (southwest of today's Chaoxian County, Anhui Province), where he was captured by Tang's troops. He was exiled there until his death.

After ousting Jie, Tang continued to eradicate the remaining forces of the Xia Dynasty. Around 1600 BC, Tang officially founded the Shang Dynasty (c. early 17th-11th century BC), the second slave regime in Chinese history.

《 Yi Yin, a slave of Shang Tang's wife, turned out to be a great aide during his campaign to topple the Xia Dynasty.

⊙ Famous Minister Yi Yin

Yi Yin was once a slave. As he was good at cooking, he took the chance of serving food to the King Shang to present his proposal how to overthrow the Xia Dynasty and build a new country. Later, he was appointed as the "Yin," namely the Right Prime Minister. In the early stage of the Shang Dynasty, he instituted a series of rites and regulations, hence establishing a stable and prosperous country. After his death, the third emperor of the Shang Dynasty Woding held a stately funeral only for the emperors for him and mourned him for three years to praise his contributions to the Shang Dynasty.

# PANGENG MOVES THE CAPITAL

From its beginning to its fall, the Shang Dynasty lasted over 500 years. Since Yin (today's Anyang, Henan Province) served as its capital for the last 270 years of the dynasty, it was also referred to as the Yin Dynasty.

A king called Pangeng ordered the capital built there. A man of great vision, Pangeng felt it imperative to come up with an effective way to ease the various conflicts that had caused the decline of the Shang Dynasty. His solution was to move the capital to Yin, where people could settle down, reclaiming wasteland to develop agriculture.

The kings of the Shang Dynasty had changed the capital many times before. Pangeng, however, designated Yin as the dynasty's "permanent capital," ruling out any possibility of moving again. The decision spoke of the growing importance of agriculture over animal herding, and people's eagerness to settle down to a more secure life. With fertile farmland and relatively few natural disasters, Yin was a good place for farming. At the same time, by moving to a new place, dynastic rulers could leave behind forces of opposition, thus enhancing political stability. That was why Pangeng strongly advocated the idea of the move.

However, many people, mainly

△ Wuding gets a talented prime minister in Mount Taihang. After Pangeng, Wuding, the 22nd king of the Shang Dynasty, led the kingdom to its peak. He once conferred the surname "Fu" upon a talented slave called "Yue" he had found in the mountain, and later promoted him to prime minister.

wealthy slave owners, were opposed to Pangeng's proposal, fearing the end of their self-indulgent life in the new capital. The king then summoned the slave owners to a meeting, during which he delivered two speeches. The first was one of kind persuasion, telling them of the advantages of the move.

"I will protect and take care of you as my ancestors did," he said, "Now I wish to lead you to a secure and merry place. But if you do not follow me wholeheartedly, the spirits of the deceased kings will punish you and bring misfortune down on you."

In the second speech, he threatened the slave owners in harsh tones. He warned all of them that they were required to abide by his directives or

⌃ Pangeng delivering a speech before moving the capital. By using a carrot-and-stick approach, he persuaded slave owners in the capital to move with him to Yin, which helped revitalize the Shang Dynasty.

otherwise be subjected to severe sanctions.

Using this carrot-and-stick approach, Pangeng succeeded in persuading the slave owners in the capital to move to Yin. There, slaves were forced to work day and night to build Yin into a prosperous metropolis. With Yin serving as its permanent capital, the Shang Dynasty enjoyed political stability and rapid social, economic and cultural progress. Pangeng's resolute decision led to the revival of the declining Shang Dynasty.

# KING WENWANG SCOUTS FOR TALENT

Ji Chang was the king of Zhou, a tributary state in the Shang Dynasty, commonly referred to as King Wenwang of Zhou. A suspicious tyrant, King Zhouwang, the last sovereign of the Shang, who reigned from 1075 to 1046 BC, feared that the regional lords with large numbers of troops under their control could pose a threat to him. He lured Ji Chang and other kings to Chaoge (today's Qixian County, northern Henan Province), a secondary capital of Zhouwang, and imprisoned them.

Boyikao, Ji Chang's son, went to rescue his father but was killed in Chaoge. Heartbroken, his younger brother Ji Fa was determined to quickly rescue his father by any means. He finally succeeded after bribing Zhouwang with many trea-

⌃ Duke Jiang.

⌄ King Wenwang meeting Duke Jiang by the Weishui River.

sures and pretty young women, while humbly pleading with him. Thus his father was saved. Later, Ji Fa became the first monarch of the Western Zhou Dynasty — King Wuwang.

Returning home, mindful of his son's death and the cruelty of Zhouwang, King Wenwang resolved to practice good governance in his state to improve it, biding the time when it could be powerful enough to topple the tyrant. However, he lacked a good aide competent in both civil administration and military tactics.

A relic site in Qixian County, Henan Province, where King Wenwang was held prisoner, and where he wrote *The Book of Changes* during his seven years of captivity; the Chinese classic explores the mysteries of the universe and the changes in the human world.

One night, he dreamt of the Heavenly God with a white-haired, white-bearded old man. "Allow me to bestow a good teacher and aide to you," the Heavenly God said to him. "His name is Wang." As he and the old man fell down on their knees to thank the Heavenly God, he woke up.

Later, before going out hunting one morning, Wenwang asked the imperial astrologer to divine what would happen to him. After performing the divination, the astrologer sang to this effect: "Go hunting by the Weishui River, and you shall make a great discovery. You will come across a wise man there, who you should make the duke. He is the very person sent by Heaven to help you." Following the clue contained in the song, Ji Chang, accompanied by a large escort, went to Panxi Stream of the Weishui River.

By the stream, he saw a silver-bearded man fishing quietly. He was exactly the old man in his dream, in terms of both looks and manner. Descending from his chariot, Ji Chang walked over to him and greeted him politely. Incognito, the king talked with him for a long time about a wide range of topics from governance to folk customs. They were so engrossed in their conversation that they forgot the passage of time. Wenwang realized that the old man before him was the capable, learned aide that he had been

scouting for. He then asked him to mount his chariot while he himself served as the driver. When they returned, Wenwang appointed him imperial mentor, calling him Duke Wang.

Surnamed Jiang, Duke Wang was also known as Duke Jiang. An eminent scholar, he had long dreamed of serving the nation. However, before meeting Wenwang, he had spent half his lifetime in poverty and obscurity. With Duke Wang's assistance, Wenwang conquered several hostile states in the vicinity of Zhou, extending the state boundaries to Hanshui, a tributary of the Yangtze River. After capturing two thirds of all China, warriors of the Zhou State were now poised to take Chaoge.

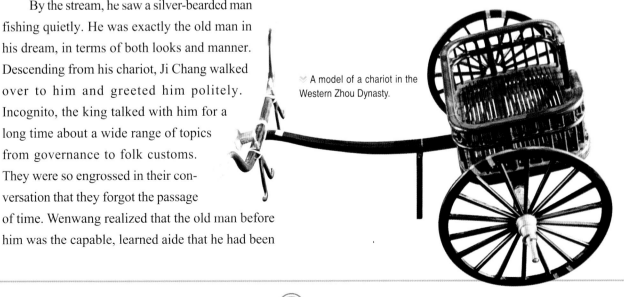

A model of a chariot in the Western Zhou Dynasty.

Five Thousand Years of Chinese Nation

# KING WUWANG TOPPLES THE SHANG DYNASTY

Corruption in the Shang Dynasty reached its peak during the reign of King Zhouwang. He had a luxurious palace built in Chaoge called "Lutai," or Deer Terrace, which served as a storehouse for the treasures he had seized. The king used various brutal methods to suppress the people. One of the devices, dubbed *paoluo*, was said to be a hollow bronze column, some 6 meters high and 2.4 meters across, stuffed with burning carbon, with three holes distributed evenly from top to bottom. Those who opposed him, officials and common people alike, would all be arrested and burned to death on the red-hot column.

As the Shang Dynasty declined, a state named Zhou was rising to the west. In stark contrast to Zhouwang's cruelty, King Wenwang of Zhou adopted a policy of "enriching the people," to encourage them to become rich through labor. Hardworking and living a simple life, the king often went to work in the fields together with the peasants to learn about their lives. By the time his son, King Wuwang (r. 1046 to 1042 BC), took the throne, Zhou had overpowered the Shang. Many states that had been subordinate to Shang turned instead to Zhou.

When Wuwang commanded his troops to advance toward Mengjin, taking with him on a chariot a memorial tablet for his late father, he was joined by many other regional rulers who had long resented Zhouwang. They all suggested to Wuwang that he should attack Chaoge directly, to end the rule of Zhouwang. After studying the in-

telligence reports filed by the spies he had sent to Chaoge, Wuwang decided that the time was not yet ripe for the final attack. He then withdrew his troops, and continued to make preparations while biding his time.

Upon learning that Wuwang's troops were nearby, Zhouwang hastened to gather about 170,000 troops to confront the invaders at Muye. Though outnumbering Wuwang's troops, Zhouwang's troops were mostly composed of slaves who had just been captured. These slaves were all outraged by the cruel king, but they were placed in the front, with elite forces and imperial guards from behind forcing them to charge, an arrangement that only heightened their desire to rebel. As soon as the battle commenced, they switched allegiances and joined soldiers from the Zhou and fought against the Shang troops. As a result, Zhouwang suffered a severe defeat at Muye. Upon seeing the fall of his dynasty, he dressed himself up, mounted the Deer Terrace, piled beautiful jade and

other precious treasures all around himself, and ordered the terrace to be set on fire, putting an end to
his wicked life.

Five days after the decisive battle at Muye,
Wuwang proclaimed the founding of the Zhou
Dynasty, taking Haojing (southeast of today's
Lintong, Shaanxi Province) as the capital. It was

⌃ Led by King Wuwang and Duke Jiang, Zhou troops defeated King
Zhouwang's army in Muye; after the battle, King Wuwang gradually
seized the territories of the Shang Dynasty.

known as the Western Zhou (1046-771 BC), the
third and last slave dynasty in Chinese history, after the Xia and Shang dynasties, and considered the
golden age of early China.

# ZHOUGONG, A LOYAL AIDE

Ji Dan, known through history as "Zhougong," was a son of King Wenwang and a brother of King Wuwang.

After toppling the Shang Dynasty, King Wuwang divided the vast territory into fiefdoms, each of which was governed as a separate state. After this had been accomplished, Wuwang, now the king of the Western Zhou Dynasty, hoped to see an end to all wars and chaos. As soon as he returned to the capital, he ordered the horses in the army to be released and the weapons put away in storehouses, a sign of long-lasting peace.

Despite this, he still remained haunted by a sense of insecurity, as there were many people who refused to obey the rulers of the Zhou Dynasty. For example, Boyi and Shuqi claimed to prefer starving to death to eating the food provided by Zhou authorities. Jizi sailed to (what

A bronze wine container of the Western Zhou Dynasty.

is now) Korea, to flee Zhou's rule; enough was enough. Obviously the rule of Wuwang was not stable. He was extremely concerned about the future of the dynasty, as he himself was feeble and aged, whereas his son, Song, was still too young to succeed him. He grew so anxious that he became seriously ill. On his sickbed, the dying king asked Duke Zhougong to help Prince Song to govern the country.

Zhougong was the fourth son of King Wenwang. Wenwang's eldest son Boyikao had been killed by King Zhouwang of the Shang Dynasty. His second and third sons were Wuwang and Guanshuxian, respectively. Guanshuxian believed that Wuwang, who had ascended the throne because Boyikao had died so young, was expected to pass the throne to him, rather than the younger Zhougong. He tried to persuade other brothers to rally together in opposition to Zhougong.

In order to relieve his brothers of their worries, Zhougong confided: "I offered to help govern the country because I do not want to see regional rulers turn against us. Now that Wenwang has died before Chengwang (Princess Song's official name after ascending the throne) has grown up, I have no choice but to shoulder the responsibility of strengthening the rule of the Zhou Dynasty."

A bronze food container of the Western Zhou Dynasty.

was then known as Zongzhou. The two city complexes were joined together, stretching some 500 kilometers. When Chengwang came of age, Zhougong returned state power to him and became his minister.

Zhougong assisted Wuwang in conquering the Shang Dynasty, and Chengwang in governing the country. He also suppressed rebellions in the east, and built Luoyi into a prosperous imperial city. For these remarkable achievements, he goes down in Chinese history as one of the most loyal ministers.

After the family feud was resolved, Zhougong led the army to the east of the country and ended the turmoil there in less than three years. He also built an imperial city called Chengzhou, west of Luoyi, which served as an important city where the king could summon regional rulers in the east to meetings and as a fort to defend the capital city. The capital, with Fengjing and Haojing at the center,

In a bid to strengthen the rule of the Zhou Dynasty, Zhougong suggested building an east capital, called Luoyi, otherwise known as Chengzhou, to house the disruptive loyalists of the Shang Dynasty. In this picture, technicians are determining the location of the new capital by using a sundial.

# KING YOUWANG TRICKS REGIONAL LORDS

When King Youwang was enthroned in the late Western Zhou Dynasty, the dynasty was at the brink of collapse, with lingering disasters and famines. Youwang, however, only continued to indulge himself in dissolute living.

Baosi, his favorite concubine, seldom ever smiled. The king used all kinds of ways to tease her hoping she would burst into laughter, but to no avail. He then announced that he would award a thousand silver coins to anyone who could make Baosi smile.

Guo Shifu, a high-ranking court official, always excelled at pleasing the king. He offered Youwang a notorious suggestion — that he could play a trick on the regional lords by sending false emergency signals.

In an effort to cope with possible attacks from the Quanrong tribe to the west, the Zhou Dynasty had built every few kilometers a total of over twenty signal towers on Lishan Mountain near Haojing. In case of attack, the soldiers defending the towers were to light fires to inform each other. When regional lords saw the fires, they would send troops to rescue the capital city.

Youwang and Baosi came to Lishan Mountain and ordered fires lit to signal the towers. Believing the capital to be under attack, nearby regional lords rushed to the rescue with their troops. They were all bewildered upon arrival, as they could not see a single invader, but only heard the sounds of merrymaking wafting from the palace in the mountain. Seeing the lords making such a great fuss, Baosi broke into laughter. When they realized that it was all a hoax, the frustrated "rescuers" angrily departed.

Youwang became so fond of Baosi that he made her the queen and her son the crown prince, after deposing Queen Shen and her son Prince Bofu. Upon learning this news, the queen's father, who ruled the fief of Shen, rose up in collaboration with Quanrong against the king. In 771 BC, Quanrong warriors besieged Haojing. The panicking king ordered fires lit at the signal towers. However, remembering the king's earlier dirty trick, no one came to his rescue. Sparsely defended, Haojing was soon overrun by invaders.

Youwang fled to the foot of Lishan Mountain, where he was killed. When they realized that the attack was real this time, the regional lords rushed to the capital, but it was too late. They had to negotiate with the lord of Shen and enthroned Yiju, son of Youwang, who was known as King Pingwang.

Pingwang moved the capital city to Luoyi (today's Luoyang, Henan Province), marking the end of the Western Zhou, and the beginning of the Eastern Zhou Dynasty (770-256 BC). The Eastern Zhou Dynasty was divided into the Spring and Autumn Period (770-476 BC) and the Warring States Period (476-256 BC), during which feuding states contended with each other against the backdrop of a weak central authority.

The Spring and Autumn Period was characterized by unrelenting wars and drastic social changes. It was said that there were over 140 states at the beginning of this period. After years of battles and annexation, only a handful of powerful states survived. These major powers continued to fight against each other for dominance. The five regional rulers who eventually established dominance were known as the "Five Overlords of the Spring and Autumn Period."

One version of the list of Overlords is: Duke Huangong of the Qi State, Duke Xianggong of the Song State, Duke Wengong of the Jin State, Duke Mugong of the Qin State, and King Zhuangwang of the Chu State. Another version is: Duke Huangong of the Qi State, Duke Wengong of the Jin State, King Zhuangwang of the Chu State, King Helu of the Wu State, and King Goujian of the Yue State.

∨ Sending false emergency signals to trick regional lords.

# DUKE HUANGONG PROMOTES A FORMER ENEMY

⌃ Guan Zhong.

Guan Zhong (?-645 BC) was a prominent statesman, strategist and military reformer in the Spring and Autumn Period. His given name was Yiwu, and Zhong was his style name. He was also known as Guan Jingzhong. Guan Zhong was a descendant of the Ji family, of the same origins as the ruling family of the Zhou Dynasty. With his remarkable wisdom, he helped Duke Huangong of the Qi State become the first overlord of the Spring and Autumn Period.

Born to a poor family, Guan Zhong worked hard when he was young, gaining a good mastery of Chinese classics such as *The Book of Songs* and *The Classic of History*. He possessed graceful manners, a wide range of knowledge and excellent martial skills. He and his close friend Bao Shuya served as mentors for princes Jiu and Xiaobai respectively.

In 686 BC, or the 12th year of the reign of Duke Xianggong of Qi, the state was plunged into chaos when Gongsun Wuzhi seized the throne after assassinating the duke. After Gongsun was killed in the following year, the two princes, who had been in exile, vied to return to their country to ascend the throne. In an effort to help Jiu beat his rival, Guan ambushed Xiaobai on the way, and shot him. However, the arrow hit a bronze pendant on his clothing. By feigning death, Xiaobai arrived at the capital first and assumed power with the help of Bao Shuya. He was posthumously titled Duke Huangong of Qi, a powerful ruler in Chinese history.

After becoming duke, Huangong managed to kill Jiu. He was plotting to slaughter Guan Zhong to seek revenge, when Bao Shuya gave him some

crucial counsel that he should forget the old grievance for the sake of the state. Bao insisted that Guan Zhong, a talented person, should be appointed to an important post in the court. Following his advice, Huangong invited Guan Zhong to Qi, and nominated him as prime minister, leaving the state in his hands. In this position, Guan Zhong made the most of his abilities.

At first, Guan Zhong suggested to Huangong that he should be friendly with neighboring states, pursue development at home before branching out, and bide his time. Unfortunately, Huangong ignored him. The duke launched a reckless attack against the State of Lu the following year, and was defeated in the battle of Changshao.

After the defeat, Guan Zhong initiated a series of reforms with a view to elevating the people,

enriching the state and strengthening its military force. Due to the reforms, the Qi State rose rapidly. He then put forward a strategy that he believed would help Huangong gain dominance over China's Central Plains: "Respect the King, and resist the barbarians."

In this slogan, the "King" referred to the king of the Zhou Dynasty. At a time when tributary states continuously battled each other under a powerless central government, Guan Zhong believed that Huangong would be able to take the moral high ground by recognizing the king's authority and to head the alliance of states in the name of the king. "The barbarians" referred to the Di and Rong people in north China. Taking advantage of the chaos, these peoples frequently beleaguered the Central Plains, posing a severe threat to all states. If he took the initiative in fighting "the barbarians," Huangong would gain the respect of other states, according to Guan Zhong.

In 652 BC, or the 34th year of the reign of Duke Huangong, King Huiwang of Zhou died. Huangong, together with other regional lords, enthroned Prince Zheng, who was known as King Xiangwang. When he took power, Xiangwang sent sacrificial meat to Huangong to honor his contribution. Huangong then summoned all the regional lords to a grand award presentation ceremony in Kuiqiu (near today's Kaocheng, Henan Province). At Guan Zhong's suggestion, these regional rulers signed a treaty, forming an alliance led by Duke Huangong.

By this time, Duke Huangong, as head of the alliance of states, had become the unchallenged overlord. All this would have been impossible without Guan Zhong. So he called this great aide, "Godfather," as a show of respect.

《 In 636 BC, soldiers of the Qi State led by Duke Huangong were crusading against the Rong troops, in collaboration with the Yan State, when in a valley they lost all sense of direction. Guan Zhong suggested that old horses might guide them out. The suggestion worked, with the troops finally traveling out of the valley by following several old horses.

# CHONG'ER ASCENDS THE THRONE AFTER 50 YEARS OF EXILE

In the rivalry for domination during the Spring and Autumn Period, Duke Wengong of the Jin State was the true successor of Duke Huangong of Qi as an overlord. Wengong, named Chong'er, was a son of Duke Xiangong of Jin.

When the queen died, Xiangong made his favorite concubine Liji the new queen. In a bid to crown her son Xiqi, Liji managed to kill the crown prince Shensheng and also attempted to murder Chong'er and Yiwu. The two princes were forced into exile. After Xiangong died, Yiwu returned and assumed power in 650 BC, calling himself Duke Huigong. Fearing that Chong'er would challenge his dukedom, Huigong sent his men to slay him.

Chong'er had been in exile in the Di State for some twelve years after leaving Jin. He had with him many of the top intellects of Jin, such as Hu Mao, Hu Yan, Zhao Cui and Jie Zitui. On hearing that Chong'er was being pursued by murderers, the father of Hu Mao and Hu Yan immediately warned him. Chong'er fled to Qi as soon as he received this report.

As soon as he arrived, Duke Huangong sent envoys to greet him. The duke treated him generously. He even married a beautiful girl named Qijiang to him. The grateful Chong'er stayed in Qi for seven years. He did not leave the state until 643 BC, when Qi started to decline with the death of Huangong. Chong'er then sought refuge in the Cao State and later found himself in the Song State.

Unfortunately, Song, which had yet to recover from a defeat by the Chu State not long before, was unable to help him. He continued his journey seeking refuge, arriving in Chu, where King Chengwang received him as a head of state.

When Duke Mugong of the Qin State sent for him in Chu, Chong'er decided to go to Qin, since he believed that the powerful state might help him return to Jin. Mugong was so kind to him that he remarried his daughter Huaiying to him. In 636 BC a formidable force from Qin escorted Chong'er to the Yellow River, which served as the boundary between Qin and Jin. Dwarfed by their enemies, the Jin soldiers surrendered quickly. Duke Huaigong was killed shortly after he fled from the capital city. Chong'er became the duke of Jin with the support of all top civil and military officers.

Chong'er, who started his exile at the age of 13, did not ascend the throne until he was 62. During the long period of exile, he and his followers had wrought strong character while broadening their vision and political wisdom. As a duke, he underscored the importance of improving domestic governance, developing the economy and restoring public confidence. As Jin rose to prosperity, Chong'er turned himself into another overlord in the Spring and Autumn Period.

» During the long exile, Chong'er and his followers strengthened their resolve and became more capable in running a state.

# KING ZHUANGWANG: FROM INACTIVE REGENT TO OVERLORD

In an attempt to dominate China's Central Plains, Duke Wengong of Jin waged an attack against Chu in Chengpu (southwest of today's Juancheng, Shandong Province, or near Chenliu, Henan Province). Defeated in battle, Chu was temporarily deprived of the chance to seek dominance.

King Zhuangwang took over the reins of Chu after King Muwang died. While the state was pre-occupied with mourning its late king, Jin summoned the regional rulers to a meeting to form a new alliance. Later, it regained influence over states such as Chen and Zheng, which the Chu State had won over. Outraged top officials in Chu vowed to fight a duel with Jin. But King Zhuangwang remained totally indifferent.

One day, Wu Ju, a senior minister, called upon the king with a riddle. "I have come to request Your Majesty's assistance to explain something that has puzzled me for a long time," he said. "There is a giant, colorful pheasant in the capital of Chu. Strangely, the bird has been inactive and silent for exactly three years. Nobody in the court knows the reason. May I venture to ask you what kind of bird it is?"

Knowing well what Wu was actually speaking of, Zhuangwang replied: "I have the answer. The bird is far from ordinary. Despite its inactivity over the past three years, it will soar high up to the skies once it takes a leap. Despite its silence over the past three years, it will impress everyone with its melodious singing once it opens its mouth. Just wait and see!"

Wu understood the king and departed happily. As expected, Zhuangwang had his orchestra disbanded and dancing girls dismissed, resolving to succeed in his political career.

He set about improving domestic governance by employing capable politicians. While carrying out political reforms, the king re-

≪ Bronze wine vessel of Marquis Yi of Zeng, Warring States Period.

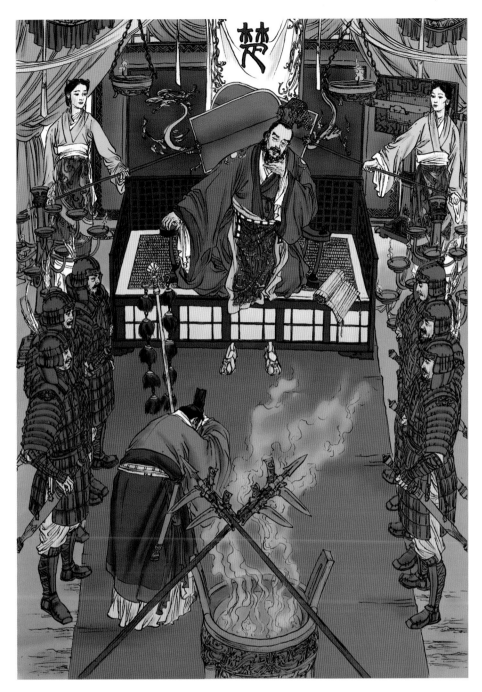

King Zhuangwang implies his determination to succeed through solving a suggestive riddle posed by a loyal minister.

King Dingwang became so frightened by this show of military might that he sent Wangsun Man, one of his ministers, to pay tribute to Zhuangwang.

When meeting the envoy, the first thing Zhuangwang asked about was how heavy were the nine tripods, huge bronze containers in the imperial ancestral temple. As nine tripods were deemed a symbol of supreme power, inquiring about their weight inferred a challenge to the king's authority. These aggressive moves boosted Chu's influence and prestige.

Several years later, Zhuangwang finally commanded his troops northward to assault Jin in defiance of its dominance. A decisive battle broke out between the two states in Bicheng. Given the lack of consensus among its squabbling commanding officers, the elite force of Jin, which boasted 600 chariots, was eliminated almost overnight.

By this time, King Zhuangwang, who had maintained low profile over three years, had risen to prominence, becoming an overlord after Duke Huangong of Qi, Duke Wengong of Jin and Duke Mugong of Qin.

cruited more troops and rigorously trained them to prepare for a major attack against Jin to avenge its defeat in Chengpu.

From the third year, when Zhuangwang took the throne, Chu won successive victories over the Yong and Song states as well as the Rong tribe. He also viewed troops along the border with the region directly administered by the king of the Zhou Dynasty.

# STRATEGIST SUN WU AND *THE ART OF WAR*

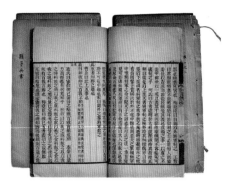

⚌ *The Art of War*, printed in the Qing Dynasty.

Sun Wu (also known honorifically as Sun Zi), the famous military theorist of the late Spring and Autumn Period, was born in the State of Qi. He later traveled to the State of Wu and was employed by King Helü. As the state gained ever greater sway and the king's grip on power further strengthened, Helü became plagued by ambitions to expand his influence abroad and seek hegemony. But he was fully aware that he must first conquer the powerful Chu State before his dream could come true.

When Sun Wu arrived in Wu, Helü received him on the recommendation of Prime Minister Wu Zixu. Doubtful about his abilities, the king asked him to conduct military training for the court ladies. Sun grouped the ladies into two teams, each headed by a favorite concubine of Helü. After giving his instructions, he ordered the ladies to start training. However, they refused to follow his orders despite repeated injunctions. He then ordered the two team leaders to be executed and appointed two new ones in their place. In the end, he succeeded in turning the delicate, pampered court ladies into well-disciplined fighters.

Although he had lost two favorite concubines, King Helü became convinced that Sun was a gifted commander. He appointed him as the general of the Wu State, charging him with duties essential to the state and its military.

In the autumn of 511 BC, Wu launched an assault against Chu. This campaign gave practical meaning to the words from *The Art of War*, "Attack him where he is unprepared, appear where you are not expected." Sun first deployed a contingent in Yicheng (southeast of today's Boxian County, Anhui Province). When Chu forces marched toward the city to wage major battle, Wu troops crossed the Huaishui River to the Qian (southeast of today's Huoxian County, Anhui Province) — Liu region (today's Liu'an City, Anhui Province). The troops withdrew again before Chu reinforcements arrived in the region.

Another contingent of Wu traveled hundreds of kilometers up the Huaishui River to besiege Xuan (today's Huangchun County, Henan Province), an important city of Chu, pretending that it planned to capture the city. However, they quickly retreated, as soon as Chu forces came to its rescue from a long way away.

The forces of Chu became so exhausted as result of the frequent, tiring deployments that their combat capacity drastically declined.

Believing the time was ripe for the final attack, Sun dispatched the well-prepared main force to quickly charge toward the enemy, to secure a great victory.

Sun Wu systematically elaborated his military strategies in his book *The Art of War*, China's oldest and best-known work on military studies. The book consists of 13 chapters, namely "Laying Plans," "Waging War," "Attack by Stratagem" "Tactical Dispositions," "Energy," "Weak and Strong Points," "Maneuvering," "Variation in Tactics," "The Army on the March," "Terrain," "The Nine Situations," "Attack by Fire" and "The Use of Spies." In this 6,000-character treatise, in addition to his insightful analysis of different wars, Sun uncovered certain universal laws of warfare. He argued that "moral laws" was the primary factor governing the art of war. He also underscored the need for a commander to be familiar with both his own army and the enemy, putting forward a universally acknowledged military rule: "If you know the enemy and know yourself, you need not fear the results of a hundred battles."

*The Art of War* goes down in the history of ancient Chinese military affairs as an invaluable masterpiece. Its author Sun Wu is thus considered the "All-time Sage of Military Studies."

⌄ Sun Wu executing the king's favorite concubines.

# KING GOUJIAN'S PERSEVERANCE

▲ Goujian.

At the end of the Spring and Autumn Period, when the states in the Central Plains were embroiled in unrelenting wars, a desperate feud broke out between the Wu and Yue states along the lower reaches of the Yangtze River. It all began with Yue's triumph over Wu in a battle, in which King Helü of Wu was slain. His successor King Fuchai vowed to take revenge, and succeeded years later when he conquered Yue and captured King Goujian. Goujian was forced to remain in Wu, suffering great humiliation, for three years before he was allowed to return home.

After returning to Yue, Goujian was committed to revitalizing his state through painstaking effort. He chose to live in harsh conditions in order to strengthen his resolve. At night, he slept on straw on the ground. Before having a meal, he would taste the gall hanging in his room, so that he would not forget his humiliations. He worked personally on the farm, while asking his wife to

▲ Pond of Swords, Huqiu, Jiangsu Province. It is said that King of Wu Helü was fond of swords. People believed he must have many high-quality swords being buried here with him after he died. So many people tried to find swords that the site was excavated into a deep pond.

Goujian tasting gall.

vade Wu. After three days of fierce battle, Yue troops seized Wu's capital and captured alive the crown prince. Hearing that his kingdom was under attack, Fuchai hastened back with his troops and sent envoys to make peace with Yue. Goujian soon pulled out his army, as he believed that Wu, still a powerful state, was unlikely to collapse easily. Four years later, Goujian launched another assault. This time, he forced Fuchai to commit suicide in Yangshang (west of today's Wuxian County, Jiangsu Province), which was besieged by Yue troops.

After seizing Wu, Goujian led his army northward across the Huaihe River. He summoned the rulers of Qi, Jin, Song and Lu states to meet in Shudi (south of today's Yingxian County, Shandong Province), where they formed an alliance. After gaining recognition from the king of the Zhou Dynasty as leader of the regional lords, Goujian became the last overlord in the Spring and Autumn Period.

weave cloth at home, thereby setting an example for Yue people to work hard to boost the state's economy and its revenue. Within a few years, the state embarked on a road to prosperity. However, in order not to arouse the suspicion of King Fuchai, Goujian continued to send envoys to frequently pay tribute to him.

In 482 BC, Fuchai and the kings of the Jin and Lu states met to form an alliance in Huangchi (southwest of present-day Fengqiu, Henan Province). Seizing this opportunity, Goujian led a 50,000-strong army to in-

Bronze sword of King Goujian of the state of Yue.

# CONFUCIUS, THE GREAT CHINESE THINKER

⩘ Confucius.

Confucius (known in China as "Kong Zi") (551-479 BC) was a native of Zouyi (southeast of present-day Qufu, Shandong Province) in Lu State in the Spring and Autumn Period, with the full name of Kong Qiu. His father, a low-ranking military officer, had died when Confucius was only three. His mother moved with him to Qufu, where he grew up. It was said that, even as a child Confucius had been keen to learn the ancient rituals. Whenever he was free, he would conduct pretend sacrificial rites using small pans and dishes.

Confucius when young was a hardworking student. He particularly revered Zhougong, who devised ancient rituals and composed music in the early days of the Zhou Dynasty. At that time, a scholar was expected to master six types of skills: rituals, music, archery, chariot driving, writing and arithmetic. Confucius possessed a superior com-

⩘ Confucius giving a lecture.

《 Dacheng Hall in the Confucius Temple.

mand of all of them.

Confucius was modest and liked learning new things. He was also skilled at handling administrative affairs. He once worked in a government storehouse. A good bookkeeper, he helped ensure an efficient, adequate supply of goods. Later, he worked as a minor official in charge of animal husbandry. Throughout his tenure, the number of cattle and sheep in the state continued rising dramatically, and all the animals were healthy and strong. Confucius thus had earned a fine reputation before he reached age 30.

Confucius started his political career at the age of 35. When Duke Zhaogong of Lu was ousted by three powerful ministers, with the family names of Jisun, Mengsun and Shusun, Confucius turned to the Qi State. When he met Duke Jinggong of Qi, he shared with him his political vision. Jinggong treated him well and considered appointing him to a high position, when Yan Ying, Prime Minster of Qi, told the duke that Confucius' ideas were disconnected from reality. As a result, Jinggong changed his mind and refused to grant him any official post.

Confucius could do nothing but return to Lu. When he was 50, he was forced to go into exile again by people who disapproved of his thinking. However, he was still anxious to obtain an opportunity to realize his political aspirations. He and his companions traveled to Wei, Cao, Song, Zheng, Chen, Cai and Chu states. Despite all the hardships on the journey and all kinds of rebuffs, he continued to promote his theories tenaciously.

Confucius was a great educator who occu-

∧ *Shijing Yuanshi* (A New Interpretation of *The Book of Songs*), by Qing-dynasty annotator Fang Yurun.

pies a significant position in the history of education in China. In slave society, only children from privileged families had access to education. Regarding this system as unfair, Confucius claimed that everybody should have the right to receive a decent education. In the private school that he founded, Confucius admitted privileged and common children alike.

It was said that Confucius had 3,000 disciples, of whom 72 stood out for their excellence. He gave lectures wherever possible — in lecture halls, in his courtyard, in his bedchamber, in the outskirts, or in horse-driven carts on journeys. A devoted teacher, he lived and worked with his students, winning deep respect from them. Confucius put forward the idea of "teaching students in accordance with their aptitude," meaning a teacher should adopt different methods to teach students with different personalities and academic levels.

In his later years, Confucius edited several important ancient Chinese classics including *The Book of Songs, Collection of Ancient Texts* and *The Spring and Autumn Annals*. After he died, his disciples compiled a 20-chapter book titled *The Analects*, based on his daily teachings and dialogues with disciples. At the same time, they spread his doctrines to an ever-wider audience, giving rise to the school of Confucianism. The main points of the Confucian philosophy may be summed up as follows:

First, Confucius set great store by the concept of "benevolence;" that is to say, rulers are expected to demonstrate concern for their subjects and refrain from overexploiting them so as to reconcile conflicts between different classes of the society. Second, he called for virtuous government and was categorically opposed to tyranny and torture. Emperor Wudi of the Han Dynasty designated Confucianism as the official ideology. For the next over 2,000 years, it served as the orthodox thinking of feudal China. The Chinese often refer to Confucius as "The Sage" to show their respect.

≪ Confucius going into retreat to become an editor of classic works after ending his abortive political career.

≫ The ancient path to the Confucius Forest. When he died in 479 BC, Confucius was buried near the Sishui River north of the town of Lu, according to historical records. Later, descendants of Confucius and their family members were also buried there, forming a cemetery known as "Confucius Forest."

≪ Confucius traveled extensively to different states.

# SHANG YANG'S REFORMS OF THE STATE OF QIN

⌃ Shang Yang. The great reformer was originally named Gongsun Yang. An aristocrat of the Wei State, he was also known as Wei Yang. However, he was best known as Shang Yang, since he had been granted a fiefdom called Shang, consisting of 15 towns, for his battle achievements in 340 BC. After Duke Xiaogong died, Shang Yang was framed by Qin aristocrats and executed by being fastened to four chariots and pulled apart.

The Spring and Autumn Period ended in 367 BC when three major families of Jin partitioned the state — arguably the most powerful state in the Spring and Autumn Period — into three smaller states, the Han, Zhao and Wei. China had by now moved into the Warring States Period, during which emerged the seven most powerful states — Qi, Chu, Yan, Han, Zhao, Wei and Qin, collectively known as the "Seven Warring States."

Qin, a state in western China, lagged behind its peers in the Central Plains in terms of political, economic and cultural development. In 361 BC, Duke Xiaogong of Qin assumed power, resolving to vitalize his state by seeking out talented personnel. He issued an order declaring: "Anyone able to devise ways for the Qin State to prosper, be he a native of Qin or a migrant from another state, shall be given an official post."

The result was that many capable people surged into Qin answering the call of Xiaogong. Among them was an aristocrat of the Wei State called Gongsun Yang, who later became known as Shang Yang. Overlooked in his home country, he came to Qin and was recommended to Duke Xiaogong.

"In order to make a country prosperous and strong, priority should be given to developing agriculture and rewarding people for their service," he told the duke during their meeting. "Reward and punishment are both indispensable to good governance. With reward and punishment, the court maintains its authority, making it easy to carry out reforms."

Completely agreeing with Shang Yang, the duke nominated him as chief advisor. He then drafted a directive to initiate reforms. However, he was unsure whether the general public would trust him and abide by the new laws.

One day, he had a 30-foot-long log erected by the south gate of the capital city and announced that anyone who could carry the log to the north gate would be rewarded with 500 grams of gold. Suspicious of Shang's announcement, nobody dared to even attempt it. Shang raised the stake to 2.5 kilograms of gold. Initially there were still no takers. But eventually a man did accomplish the task and pocketed the lavish prize. The anecdote soon spread across the country, creating a nationwide sensation. All Qin residents then were convinced that Shang Yang was a person who meant what he said.

Now that he had the people's trust, Shang Yang issued the new laws he had drafted. The laws put forward clear-cut provisions regarding reward and punishment, stipulating that battle achievements shall be taken as the sole criterion for determining the rank of officials and the nobility. Thanks to this reform, Qin underwent rapid growth in agricultural production and military influence. Shortly after, it invaded Wei from its west, overran the whole state and seized its capital.

In the beginning, Shang Yang's extensive reforms met with strong opposition from many aristocrats and ministers. They were all silenced when he meted out punishment to two mentors of a prince who had breached the law.

"The entire nation is required to abide by the

» A standard measure of one liter, adopted by Shang Yang to unify the units of measurement in the Qin State.

law," he told Duke Xiaogong. "If a prince violates the law, his mentors shall be held accountable."

Ten years later, Qin became so influential that the king of the Zhou Dynasty sent sacrificial offering of meat to Duke Xiaogong in recognition of his status and nominated him as chief of the regional lords. Rulers governing the Central Plains all extended their congratulations.

≫ Shang Yang winning the people's trust.

# RETURNING THE JADE INTACT TO ZHAO

During the Warring States Period, King Huiwenwang of the Zhao State happened to receive a piece of jade, which was named "Heshibi" (Jade Disc of He), after its finder. The jade disc was crystal clear and deemed an invaluable treasure. In 283 BC, King Zhaoxiangwang of Qin sent an envoy to Zhao, telling Huiwenwang that he was willing to trade 15 cities for the Heshibi. Huiwenwang hesitated, not knowing what to do, when someone recommended consulting Lin Xiangru.

"Fifteen cities is indeed a high price to be offered for a piece of jade," Lin said to the king, "if we do not agree, Qin may blame us for upsetting the deal. However, Qin would be to blame if it re-

⌄ Lin Xiangru threatening to smash the invaluable jade disc on a column.

A jade lantern of the Warring States Period.

lumn, jade disc in hand, as if he were about to smash it. Fearing that he would damage the disc, Zhaoxiangwang apologized to him and showed him on a map the 15 cities that he said he would present to Zhao.

"Before sending the jade to you, the King of Zhao fasted for five days. He also held a grand ceremony in the main palace to part with the jade. If you are sincere, you should also fast for five days and hold a jade-reception ceremony in your main palace, where I would be glad to present the jade disc to you."

Zhaoxiangwang consented. After returning to his lodgings, Lin asked one of his valets to dress up as a merchant and take the jade disc back to Zhao along an unknown route.

Five days later, Zhaoxiangwang and his ministers were waiting in the main palace where a pompous ceremony was to be held to receive the jade disc, when Lin appeared. "I have fasted for five days," claimed the king, "now show me the jade."

"Since Duke Mugong, there have been no honest rulers in the Qin State," replied Lin, "I was afraid that I might be deceived and fail the King of Zhao. So I have sent back the jade. I beg for your punishment, Your Majesty."

Upon hearing these remarks, Zhaoxiangwang flew into a rage. "A universally acknowledged truth is that the strong can bully the weak, rather than the other way round," argued Lin. "If Your Majesty truly likes that piece of jade, you can cede 15 cities to Zhao first, and then send an envoy with me to fetch it. After acquiring the cities, the King of Zhao shall not dare to keep the jade from you."

fused to hand over the cities after receiving the jade. In my opinion, it is better we agree to the deal and allow Qin to shoulder the blame."

"Then, I shall have to trouble you to take the jade to Qin," the king said, "but what if Qin breaks the promise?"

"If it hands over the cities, I will leave the jade there," replied Lin, "otherwise, I shall bring it back safe and sound."

Shortly after Lin arrived in Xianyang, the capital of Qin, King Zhaoxiangwang received him in a minor palace. Lin presented the Heshibi to the king, who examined it appreciatively for quite some time, before passing it onto his ministers and concubines. All of them were most amazed. The palace was soon filled with cheering. However, Zhaoxiangwang did not mention the cities.

"The jade disc has a small flaw, Your Majesty," Lin said as he approached the king, "allow me to show you."

As soon as he took back the jade disc, he exclaimed angrily, with eyes wide open: "You were not at all sincere about the deal. That is why I have taken back the jade disc. If you dare to take it away by force, I shall knock my head on the column and smash the disc too."

He walked toward the co-

A round flat piece of jade with designs of Chinese dragons and phoenixes.

Lin talked so confidently and eloquently that Zhaoxiangwang found it inappropriate to turn hostile. "We had better allow Lin Xiangru to return to Zhao," he lamented. From then on, the king no longer brought up the cities-for-jade deal any more.

# JING KE ATTEMPTS TO ASSASSINATE THE KING OF QIN

⌃ A terracotta archer from Qin Shi Huang's Mausoleum.

Prince Dan of the State of Yan during the Warring States Period had been a hostage in the Qin State before he secretly fled back to Yan. Furious at Qin, he was keen to take revenge. Using all his wealth, he scouted for people who could assassinate Ying Zheng, King of Qin. Later, he was introduced to a competent warrior named Jing Ke. He took him in as a protégé and treated him well. Jing, of course, was grateful to the prince.

One day in 230 BC, Dan said to Jing Ke: "I am considering sending a warrior to the King of Qin disguised as an envoy. He should try to force the king to return to the other states all the lands he has occupied. If he does not consent, the warrior should assassinate him. What do you think of this idea?"

"Not bad," answered Jing, "but we must convince the king that we are there to make peace before we would be allowed to approach him. I hear that the king has long been coveting the fertile Dukang region of Yan. Also, Fan Yuqi, a Qin general who the King of Qin is offering a bounty for, has taken refuge in Yan. I am certain the king will meet me personally if I were to visit him with Fan's head and a map of Dukang. Then I shall be able to do something about him."

Vexed, the prince mused, "It is easy to prepare a map of Dukang, but how can I hurt General Fan, who turned to me to avoid the persecution of Qin?"

Knowing that Dan could not bear to have Fan executed, Jing met the general privately and told him everything. "All right, take my head with you," Fan said resolutely, before beheading himself with a sword.

Dan prepared a sharp dagger, which had been boiled in poisonous liquid to immediately kill those stabbed with it. He gave this dagger to Jing Ke as the weapon to assassinate the King of Qin. He also designated 13-year-old Qin Wuyang as his assistant.

In 227 BC, Jing Ke set off toward Xianyang, the capital of Qin. Dan, clad in white robes and a white hat, saw him off by the Yishui River.

The King of Qin was overjoyed to learn that an envoy from Yan had brought both the head of Fan Yuqi and the map of Dukang. He decided to meet him in Xianyang Palace. During the meeting, the young Qin Wuyang became so nervous that his legs began to tremble.

"This is the first time this rustic has witnessed Your Majesty's imposing charisma," Jing Ke explained with a smile, "No wonder he is frightened.

《 Jing Ke attempting to assassinate the King of Qin.

Please do not mind him."

However, the king grew suspicious. "Let Qin Wuyang hand the map to you and come to me by yourself," he said to Jing.

Taking the map from Qin Wuyang, he approached close to the king and first presented him a wooden box. Opening the box, the king saw the head of Fan Yuqi. He then asked Jing to show him the map. Jing scrolled out the map slowly until the dagger that had been hidden in the map appeared. He then grabbed the dagger and stabbed at the king's chest.

At this critical moment, a doctor attending to the king threw his medicine chest at Jing Ke. While Jing fended off the medicine chest with his hand, the king took out his sword and hit him in the left leg. Jing staggered and fell to the ground. He then threw his dagger at the king but missed him. The king jabbed with his sword at the empty-handed Jing Ke several times, before his bodyguards rushed to his rescue and slew the assassin.

》 A bronze sword of the Warring States Period.

# THE FIRST EMPEROR

With the success of Shang Yang's reforms, Qin grew ever more powerful. Several generations later, Ying Zheng, the King of Qin, finally unified China by conquering all the other six states in 221 BC. Ying Zheng believed that there would be no difference between him and the kings of the six states he had overthrown if he were to continue using the title of "King." So he decided to adopt a new title, and dubbed himself "Emperor," after the legendary sovereigns of prehistoric China, proclaiming himself as "Shi Huang Di," ("First Emperor"). He was therefore called "Qin Shi Huang" in history. From then on, "Emperor" replaced "King" to become the title of the supreme ruler in China.

Qin Shi Huang divided his empire into 36 commanderies, under which counties were set up. Each commandery was governed by three officials directly appointed by the Central Government: a governor, military governor, and supervisor. The governor was the chief executive of a commandery, responsible for all its major affairs. The military governor was responsible for local public security while serving as the commander of the armed forces in the commandery. The supervisor was in charge of informing the Central Government about the local implementation of central policies, reporting on the governors' exercise of power.

In the Central Government, the First Emperor created a series of important posts such as prime minister, censor general, imperial minister of defense, chamberlain for law enforcement and clerk of the capital for supplies — high-ranking officials who were expected to assist the emperor in governing the country. This political system featuring central dictatorship established by Qin Shi Huang had far-reaching implications in Chinese history.

At the same time, Qin Shi Huang announced that the Qin State's round bronze coins with square holes, with a standard weight of 25 grams, should be used across the country, rendering invalid the currencies of the other six states. The emperor also ordered standardization of the units of weights and measurements. In order to facilitate the spread of government policies and laws, as well as to promote cultural exchange, he unified the Chinese script, designating "Xiaozhuan," or the seal script, as the standard script. Later, "Lishu," literally "official script," which was easier to write than "Xiaozhuan," was developed based on popular writing habits. Lishu was quite similar to "Kaishu," or the regular script, widely used today.

The series of measures that Qin Shi Huang took, such as abolishing of the fief system, and unifying the currency, units of weights and measurements and the script, were conducive to cementing unification and promoting social, economic and cultural development. These should all be deemed remarkable contributions made by the emperor.

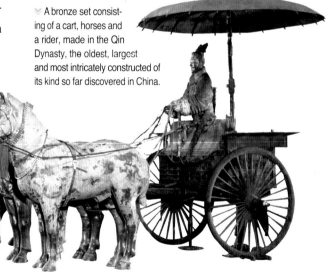

⩔ A bronze set consisting of a cart, horses and a rider, made in the Qin Dynasty, the oldest, largest and most intricately constructed of its kind so far discovered in China.

The First Emperor who unified China.

# CONSTRUCTING THE GREAT WALL

△ Head of a terracotta warrior dating back to the Qin Dynasty.

In the early days, after China had been unified by the powerful Qin State, its northern frontiers were often plagued by nomadic people, especially the Huns.

In 215 BC, Qin Shi Huang deployed a 300,000-strong army commanded by General Meng Tian to resist the Huns, and recover the lands occupied by them. Despite this, the threat from the Huns persisted. In a bid to strengthen national defense and safeguard the Central Plains, the emperor decided to connect and reinforce the earlier fortifications of the Yan, Zhao and Qin states and build fortresses at strategic points, thus forming a defensive barrier along China's northern border to keep the Huns at bay.

General Meng Tian was put in charge of this project. He led the 300,000 soldiers deployed to fight against the Huns, to build the Great Wall. At the same time, he recruited many more laborers from all over the country. They worked all day and all night, quarrying stones from mountains and transporting brick and clay. The project lasted over a decade, during which numerous laborers died from the backbreaking toil. However, without the Great Wall, residents living in the Central Plains would have suffered the scourge of war once the Huns invaded. Bearing this in mind, Meng strictly oversaw the progress of the project.

The Great Wall ran across from what is today's Lintao, Gansu Province, to eastern Liaoning Province, a distance of over 5,000 kilometers. It was built through the mountains of northern China, following the contours of the terrain. The wall itself rose lower on sheer mountainsides, but could be as high as 10 meters where the land was flat and level.

The wall had an intricate structure. The wall itself was made of rammed loess, which was very solid. Along its top was a parapet wall with holes through which soldiers could keep watch for the enemy in hiding. The Great Wall was dotted with strongholds, which served as watchtowers. In addition, signal towers

⊙ Burn Books and Bury Confucian Scholars Alive

In 213 BC, according to the proposal of Li Si, Qin Shi Huang (the first emperor of the Qin Dynasty) ordered: except the history books by the State Qin and books about medicine, divination and agriculture, all books, including those history books by other states, copies of *The Book of Songs* and *The Book of Documents*, and works of various schools, should be burnt off. Furthermore in 212 BC, Qin Shi Huang ordered to bury many Confucian scholars alive. Excusing that the alchemists and Confucian scholars Lu and Hou libeled him and spread fallacies to deceive people, the emperor ordered to bury over 460 Confucian scholars and alchemists alive out of the Xianyang City (today's Xi'an).

were built at strategic points. When they saw any sign of approaching enemies, the soldiers would light fires to signal each other so that all the frontier troops could be informed of the situation and prepare to fight the invaders.

Over a long period of time, the Great Wall served as a defense work against the hostile nomads to the north, helping to safeguard the agricultural economy in China's Central Plains. A number of later dynasties also constructed walls for the same purpose, the most famous of which was the Great Wall of the Ming Dynasty. Today, the Great Wall is more often regarded as a magnificent cultural heritage that the ancient Chinese left to the world.

⌃ A large tile from the Qin Dynasty.

≪ Building the Great Wall.

# HONGMEN BANQUET

Soon after the death of Qin Shi Huang in 209 BC, his Prime Minister Zhao Gao manipulated the coronation of Hu Hai, the dead emperor's second son. That same year saw the outbreak of China's first massive peasant insurrection. It all began

△ Zhang Liang.

when the convicts Chen Sheng and Wu Guang defiantly questioned the legitimacy of an autocratic government by asking, "Are the nobility born noble?" The six-month-long revolt they led delivered a deadly blow to the political façade of the Qin Dynasty, already crippled by the corruption of its officials and the follies of its monarch, paving the way for its downfall. Despite the defeat of Chen Sheng and Wu Guang, uprisings against the government spread to become pandemic.

Out of the massive turmoil of the many skirmishes across the country emerged Xiang Yu and Liu Bang as the two leading forces. Instead of declaring themselves king as Chen Sheng had done, they crowned the grandson of the last prince of Chu, one of the warring states Qin had subdued. The new prince promised the principality of Qin to anyone who was the first to enter Xianyang, the imperial capital. Xiang Yu turned out to be a fierce warrior; in one of his typical battles, his troops destroyed a Qin army of 200,000. Liu Bang, however, listened to one of his top advisors, Zhang Liang, and adopted a more benign strategy focused on winning over his opponents through peaceful means. This strategy paid off. Liu Bang avoided all the violent encounters Xiang Yu was forced to fight through, and thus ended up in Xianyang before his rival. In 206 BC the emperor of the Qin surrendered to Liu Bang, marking the end of his dynasty.

Xiang Yu was furious when he learnt that Liu Bang had beaten him to the Qin lands. His generals smashed their way through to penetrate Hangu Pass, a strategically important gateway to Xianyang, and encamped their troops 50 kilometers away from the capital city. An officer from Liu Bang's army sent a message to Xiang Yu, reporting that Liu Bang was going to claim the principality of Qin as well as all the treasures of the empire. Xiang Yu was enraged upon hearing these words. His advisor Fan Zeng believed Liu Bang to be capable of creating major trouble for Xiang Yu and thus had to be fought before it was too late.

However, Xiang Yu's uncle Xiang Bo was friend with Zhang Liang, who had once saved his life. He was so worried that Zhang Liang would be killed in a sudden raid by Xiang Yu that he skulked away to Liu Bang's place on a swift horse to warn Zhang Liang about the impending strike, and urged him to leave Liu Bang.

Zhang Liang refused to leave Liu Bang but instead informed him of the bad news. Liu Bang begged to be introduced to his uncle. He reassured Xiang Bo that he had never entertained the slightest notion of standing up against Xiang Yu. Xiang Bo was soon won over and agreed to speak on behalf of Liu Bang when he returned to Xiang Yu's camp. But he told Liu Bang that he must offer an apology in person to Xiang Yu.

Early the next day, Liu Bang met with Xiang Yu. Zhang Liang, his bodyguard Fan Kuai and just over 100 soldiers were with him. At the meeting, Liu Bang referred to the fact that he had worked in concert with Xiang Yu in the war on the Qin Dynasty, with each of them looking after their own theatres. He stressed that he had never expected things to work out the way they did, and how blamelessly saddened he had felt to learn Xiang Yu had listened to and become angered by the false accusations against him. His humble manner made Xiang Yu's wrath vanish. In Hongmen, where he had his headquarters, Xiang Yu invited Liu Bang to a banquet. Fan Zeng, Xiang Bo and Zhang Liang were all present. Fan Zeng repeatedly gestured to his lord, trying to remind him that he had to kill Liu Bang and had to do it now, but Xiang Yu turned his back on him. Knowing his lord would not kill the potential enemy who for the moment appeared so soft and sweet, Fan Zeng excused himself from the dinner party and spoke to Xiang Zhuang, Xiang Yu's cousin. He told Xiang Zhuang to walk in, make a toast and kill Liu Bang in his seat. Xiang Zhuang entered to make a toast and then offered to perform a sword dance, since there was not a great deal of entertainment at the military camp. Xiang Bo, who was already basically a supporter of Liu Bang in this situation, realized what was happening. So he offered to join Xiang Zhuang in the sword dance in order to confound his attempts at assassination. Seeing that things were going very wrong, Zhang Liang left the party to request Fan Kuai's assistance.

Once he was informed of the situation, Fan Kuai ran through the camp gates to rescue his lord. Xiang Yu's guards tried to stop him but Fan Kuai was too fast and too strong for them. Like a bolt of lightning he smashed open the blinds hanging over the entrance of the hut and stormed in, his hair like flames of fury and his eyes flashing with anger. Xiang Yu was surprised and rose from his seat. Hand on his sword, he demanded, "Who is this man?" Zhang Liang said this was Liu Bang's charioteer. Impressed by this formidable warrior, Xiang Yu ordered a cup of wine to be presented to Fan Kuai. After he had emptied the cup, Xiang Yu then gave him a leg of pork. Fan Kuai set down his shield on the ground, chopped the leg with his sword over it, and ate it all.

While Xiang Yu was still overcome by amazement with Fan Kuai's courage and eloquence, Liu Bang left the dinner ostensibly to relieve himself. But he had no intention of returning. Instead, he entrusted the gifts he had brought for Xiang Yu with Zhang Liang, and asked him to present them on his behalf, while he fled with Fan Kuai back to their own camp via a bypath.

⌄ At the Hongmen Banquet. Xiang Yu's costly failure to make a firm decision gives Liu Bang the chance to escape and become more powerful.

# THE DESTRUCTION OF XIANG YU

⌃ Xiang Yu.

The political vacuum left by the deposed Qin Dynasty was filled by self-styled petty princes whose power had expanded during the war, to the extent that they claimed relative independence from each other along with a fair share of the spoils. In 206 BC Xiang Yu, the commander-in-chief of the allied forces, took over authority to officially recognize this regressive feudalism by legitimizing allies' titles to princedoms or dukedoms. Xiang Yu proclaimed himself "Xi Chu Ba Wang," or the Grand King of Western Chu, with the seat of his government in Pengcheng (today's Xuzhou, Jiangsu Province). Liu Bang was among the 18 warlords whom Xiang Yu made princes; he was assigned the territories of Ba, Shu and Hanzhong. The same year saw the beginning of discord between Xiang Yu and Liu Bang vying for supremacy. The ensuing war went on for four years. In 202 BC, Liu Bang chased Xiang Yu to Guling (south of today's Taikang, Henan Province). He was joined by Han Xin, Ying Bu and Peng Yue, as they besieged Xiang Yu in Gaixia. Xiang Yu was outnumbered, yet he refused to go down easily. He still had the same elite troops he had possessed under his command from the time he had risen from his home state of Chu. Now they were cornered but they were set to fight to their last breath. Seeing that force could not break him, Zhang Liang resorted

to craft. He had his men sing the folksongs of Chu State.

The psychological warfare proved to be effective. Folksongs from their homeland distressed Xiang Yu's soldiers so severely that they no longer wanted to fight but abandoned their posts. Even Xiang Bo left his nephew for Zhang Liang. Xiang Yu was aghast when he heard the songs, which to him to mean that Liu Bang had taken his home state and drafted soldiers from there. Knowing his days were coming to an end, Xiang Yu ordered wine for his last dinner with his concubine Yu. In his hut, he expressed these tragic lines:

*I was able and I shattered the world*
*'til Fate decided my doom was due.*
*My horse sensing the time quit the race,*
*but you, O my love,*
*what shall I do with you?*

Yu joined him in chorus. Xiang Yu was in tears, as was everyone at the dinner. Then Yu killed herself. Xiang Yu mounted his horse, to attempt to flee; just over 800 cavalrymen accompanied him. They managed to break through the siege and headed southeast.

Xiang Yu and his men fought their way to Dongcheng (northwest of Tuxian, Anhui). By this time he had

only 28 cavalry with him, with thousands of enemy soldiers pursuing them. Knowing he could probably not escape, Xiang Yu said to his men: "You know that there was not a single encounter in my eight years as commander in which I did not subdue whoever stood up against me. I out-dared all other heroes in this fight for supremacy, but this seems to be how I shall go down. If this is what Fate intends for me, so be it. But it's certainly not that I am not a good fighter." Then Xiang Yu led his men into battle again. By the time they arrived at the Wujiang River (east of Taihe County, Anhui, where the river empties into the Yangtze from the west), they had lost two more companions. Now, it happened that a district governor in this neighbor-

hood had a boat moored for Xiang Yu. He urged him to board the boat and go across the river back to his home state. Xiang Yu refused to return home defeated and alone. Instead, he and his soldiers headed back into the battle with Liu Bang's men. Xiang Yu was as unyielding as a cornered lion; he and his faithful followers killed hundreds. But in the end, he killed himself with his own sword. Xiang Yu died at only 31 years of age.

⌄ Xiang Yu preferred to die, rather than take the only chance of fleeing across the river. Over a millennium later, a woman poet celebrated his character in her lines: "*His story shall be told forever / Of how he would not retreat across the river.*"

# ZHANG QIAN, ENVOY TO THE WESTERN TERRITORY

⌃ Gilded Bronze Horse. Unearthed from an unidentified tomb in Maoling, Shaanxi Province. The artwork and the fine gilding demonstrate the technical heights the Western Han Dynasty reached over 2,000 years ago.

From the day it was founded, the Han Dynasty was beleaguered by a pastoral tribe from the north called the Xiong Nu, or Huns. Little could be done to stop these exploiting invaders, until the dynasty reached its zenith during the reign of Emperor Wu Di (r. 140-188 BC). An economic recovery policy characterized by little government intervention and light taxation, as adopted by previous emperors, meant that Emperor Wu Di was financially ready to act more aggressively on the issue of national security. Apart from sending troops to fight the Xiong Nu, the emperor also started appointing ambassadors to the Western Territory, a geographical term used during the Han Dynasty to refer to the states and people inhabiting today's Xinjiang and the regions beyond the Congling Mountains (Pamirs), with the objective of eliciting an alliance in the war on the Xiong Nu. Zhang Qian (born in Hanzhong, Shaanxi) was the first government envoy dispatched to the Western Territory.

In 138 BC, a Han delegation led by Zhang Qian started traveling west from Longxi. They did not travel long before they fell into the hands of the Xiong Nu, who detained them for ten years. The Xiong Nu gave a young woman in marriage to Zhang Qian, and they had children. But Zhang Qian still never stopped thinking of his mission. At last, together with his family and a few cohorts, he managed to escape the Xiong Nu. The group traveled west across the Congling Mountains into Ferghana (Dawan). The king of Ferghana recommended Zhang Qian and his delegation to another state, Kangju, from where they moved to Tukhara.

The political situation changed in a way that did not favor a Han-Tukhara

» Zhang Qian on his diplomatic journey to the Western Region. His trip brought into being the Silk Road, a cross-continent caravan route that connected the East and the West.

alliance against the Xiong Nu. Zhang Qian spent over a year in Tukhara without ever being able to interest the king of Tukhara in what he had come to do. In 126 BC, Zhang Qian returned in Chang'an, the capital of the Han Dynasty. He had left with a delegation of over a hundred, but returned with only one partner accompanying him.

The expedition into the Western Territory took 13 years. It did not bring about an alliance with Tukhara, but it allowed Zhang Qian to learn a great deal about the lands of the Western Territory and the peoples living there. In recognition of the useful knowledge that Zhang Qian had returned with, as well as of the pioneering political groundwork he had done for future diplomacy, Emperor Wu Di promoted Zhang Qian to be superior grand master of the palace and his assistant commissioner.

⌃ Dunhuang mural: Zhang Qian, on his knees with an official tablet in his hand, on leaving Emperor Wu Di of the Western Han Dynasty.

In 119 BC, Zhang Qian started on his second trip to the Western Territory with a view to establishing diplomatic ties with Wusun. Accompanying him on the trip were 300 cohorts. They took 600 horses, 10,000 sheep and cattle, and large quantities of precious silk, which they would present to the king of Wusun when they arrived.

The king of Wusun received Zhang Qian in the same way he had received a chieftain of the Xiong Nu. But, what was considered a most elaborate and honorific reception ceremony in the local culture was not good enough for Zhang Qian, who insisted that the emperor of the Han Dynasty, whom he represented, deserved much more than a chieftain of the Xiong Nu. He told the king of Wusun: "My Emperor is the Son of Heaven. The beneficiary of whatever he confers must go down on his knees. So, either Your Lordship should kneel, or I take these presents back." After the king of Wusun obliged with the Han etiquette, Zhang Qian told him that the Han government would marry a princess to him

if the state worked together with the Han Dynasty to drive away the Xiong Nu. But, Wusun being close to the territory of the Xiong Nu while far from that of the Han Dynasty, geopolitics made the royal court of Wusun believe that making war with the Xiong Nu was very unwise. Zhang Qian was finely treated in the palace of the king of Wusun, but he could not convince the king to enter into an alliance with the Han Dynasty. All he could do in Wusun was to dispatch envoys to many other states in the Western Territory. Han representatives made it as far as the Persian Gulf. In 115 BC, Zhang Qian returned to Chang'an together with an envoy from the Wusun royal court. He died the following year. The trail that Zhang Qian blazed in his diplomatic journeys was later used by caravans as well as envoys, and came to be called the "Silk Road," a trade route across the Eurasian continent, bringing elements of Chinese culture all the way to Western Asia, and Europe.

⊙ The Silk Road

Since Zhang Qian successfully arrived at the Western Territory on a diplomatic mission, large amount of silk fabrics of China were transported into those European and Asian countries along his course to the Western Territory. This road, which is famed for its major function of transportation of China's silk products across the Asia, is commonly called Silk Road. The road connecting China, Parthia, Greece, Rome, Arab, Macedonia and some other countries played a significant role in ancient inland trades.

# SIMA QIAN, THE GREAT HISTORIOGRAPHER

Sima Qian was born in Longmen (today's Hancheng, Shaanxi Province). His father Sima Tan was a royal historiographer. At 10, Sima Qian was already well versed in history and adept with words as well.

Sima Tan died when Sima Qian was 36. On his deathbed, the old historian cried out to his son about the ambitious mission he had barely started yet had to leave unfinished, saying: "Together with the birth of the Han Dynasty has returned this Golden Age, with the throne in the hand of the righteous, and wisely served. This is a time of grandeur and nobility that a royal historiographer must bear witness to, or he would not be doing his duty. You must finish what I was able to only start, my son."

Two years later, Sima Qian succeeded his father as royal historiographer, and set out to write the history book that his father had left unfinished. Circumstances seemed to be right for him to fulfill the task when, as the royal historiographer, Sima Qian gained access to government archives as well as the rare books in the royal library. But then, tragedy struck. In the year Sima Qian was 48, an officer, Li Ling, was captured in a campaign by the Xiong Nu. When

» An illustration about "Returning the Jade Intact to Zhao" in *Shi Ji*, or *Records of the Historian*.

rumors reached the capital Chang'an that Li Ling had surrendered to the enemy, Emperor Wu Di had Li's whole family executed, which then pushed General Li toward the Xiong Nu. In a dramatic twist of events, the case involved Sima Qian, who indiscreetly spoke up in defense of Li Ling. In his wrath, Emperor Wu Di had him castrated, a punishment that was as humiliating as it was physically crippling.

Being implicated in a case of alleged treason resulted in Sima Qian being castrated, he survived the humiliation and finished *Shi Ji.*

Devastated as he was by his ill fortune, Sima Qian nevertheless managed to cast aside the idea of suicide. He decided that he had to live so that he could finish the history book his father had not been able to, being what he knew would allow the deceased histo-

Tiger-shaped base, Han Dynasty.

tises (records of important rules and rituals, astronomy as well as political and economic life), 30 Hereditary Houses (records of princes, dukes and renowned figures such as Confucius, Chen Sheng, etc.) and 70 Lives (covering all other famous personages, lives of tribes, neighboring countries, etc.). Of all these, Biographies and Lives are the most significant. Since Sima Qian introduced this genre in historiography, all later dynastic historiographers followed suit in recording history.

rian to at last rest in peace.

After years of hard work, Sima Qian finally completed the great work Shi Ji, or *Records of the Historian* when he was 53. The book, containing 130 chapters and over 520,000 characters, is divided into 12 Biographies (kings and emperors), 10 Chronicles (records of major historical events and figures in the form of table to supplement Biographies, eight Trea-

Pages from a Qing edition of *Shi Ji*, or *Records of the Historian*.

# WANG MANG THE USURPER

The military actions that Emperor Wu Di engaged in against the Xiong Nu weakened the empire both financially and politically. By the time Emperor Yuan Di ruled (48-33 BC), the governing bureaucracy, now controlled by the emperor's relatives on his mother's side, had become so corrupt that it threatened to take down the whole empire. This power shift from the emperor to his mother's family, considered dangerous and illegitimate, took place when Emperor Yuan Di died; and his son succeeded him as Emperor Cheng Di (r. 32-36 BC), and made his mother Wang Zhengjun the "Queen Mother," promoting all his maternal uncles to important positions in government.

One of the emperor's uncles had a son named Wang Mang. Wang Mang harbored major ambitions for power, and knew he must prepare himself intel-

lectually and politically for his aspirations. He spent years growing closer to his uncle Wang Feng, whom the emperor had granted military importance; so that when his uncle grew old and retired, he would be the one to succeed him. He did indeed end up succeeding Wang Feng, and power was now in his hands One other move Wang Mang had made to fulfill his ambitions involved building a support network of those who would help him when needed. He helped his friends enter the government and shared so much of

⌃ Tile carving: Green Dragon, Wang Mang's reigning period.

⌃ Tile carving: Red Bird, Wang Mang's reigning period.

⌃ Tile carving: White Tiger, Wang Mang's reigning period.

⌃ Tile carving: Black Turtle, Wang Mang's reigning period.

his fortune with them that he himself lived most frugally.

Some time after Emperor Ai Di had ascended the throne in 6 BC, Wang Mang found the gate to power was shut to him. But, after the death of Emperor Ai Di, he was again on the rise; and Wang Zhengjun, as the grandmother of the former emperor, helped him to crown Emperor Ping Di (r. AD 1-5). Wang Mang gave his daughter in marriage to the new emperor, so that, as his father-in-law, he acquired still more power and influence in the government. In AD 5, Wang Mang poisoned the 14-year-old Emperor Ping Di, his son-in-law. He then coerced his aunt, Queen Mother Wang Zhengjun, into agreeing to his managing the state affairs on behalf of the throne while the throne remained vacant. In the same year, as Wang Mang had started to rule as

"Regent," he made a 2-year-old boy from the royal family the crown prince, giving the impression that he was merely taking care of the throne for its legitimate heir until he grew up and was mature enough to take over. All he, in reality, wanted was to take over himself. So he sent a cousin to his aunt Wang Zhengjun for the official seal of the emperor. Full of emotion and indignation, the queen dowager confronted her nephew, accusing him of ungratefulness for all the Han-dynasty royal family had done for the Wang family. But the elderly lady knew she would be unable to hold onto the seal. In the end she had to surrender it, crying bitterly at the outrage.

Early in AD 9, Wang Mang crowned himself as the emperor, changing the dynastic name for the empire from Han to Xin, and officially taking over the sovereignty of what historians refer to as the Western Han Dynasty.

≪ Wang Mang takes over the emperor's seal.

# THE PEASANTS REVOLT

⌃ Stone *Pixie*, Han Dynasty. *Pixie* is a legendary animal that can ward off evil spirits. This statue is impressive for its dynamism.

The new dynasty launched a series of reforms aimed at settling the grievances and resentment felt across the empire. None of the reforms were successful. People resented Wang Mang's evil conducts and cruel suppression, and when natural disasters struck, the bankrupt peasants had nothing left to do but revolt.

Among the first to rise up against the authorities were hungry peasants digging water-chestnuts for food in the wetlands of Jingzhou in AD 17. Under their leader Wang Kuang, the rebels took over Lülin Mountain (today's Dangyang County, Hubei Province), from which they took their name. Before long, the Lülin Rebels gained control over the villages in the vicinity of their base area and within months grew in number to 7,000 to 8,000 soldiers.

The next year saw an uprising of peasants under Fan Chong in Juxian County (in today's Shandong Province). The 100,000 insurgents were known as the Red Brow Rebels, owing to the fact that they painted their eyebrows red to distinguish from their enemies in combat.

The government was weak in fighting the

insurrection. In one of their encounters, the Lülin Rebels overwhelmed government forces, killing thousands, plundering their supplies and facilities. The rebel forces took advantage of their military success and invaded three counties in Hubei Province, where they set free all the prisoners and opened the government granary to the hungry. Before long the number of rebel soldiers on Lülin Mountain had exceeded 50,000.

In AD 22, Wang Mang commissioned his Prime Minister Wang Kuang and General Lian Dan on a campaign against the Red Brow Rebels. Fan Chong engaged the government forces of 100,000 soldiers in Wuyan, Shandong Province, and destroyed

them. Prime Minister Wang Kuang escaped alive with a stab wound in his thigh, while General Lian Dan was killed in the confusion of the battle.

News of the rebel forces defying the government spread far and wide, putting ideas into the heads of desperate peasants elsewhere. Meanwhile, Liu Xiu, a landlord from Chongling, Nanyang (today's Zaoyang County, Hubei Province), built up an army of 7,000 to 8,000 rebels called the Chongling Army. The Chongling Army joined

rebel forces from Lülin Mountain and grew even bigger after they defeated several more generals of Emperor Wang Mang. In AD 25, Liu Xiu subdued all opponents and made himself emperor of the Eastern Han Dynasty (AD 25-220), with its capital in Luoyang.

⌄ The Red Brow rebels won in Wuyan.

Five Thousand Years of Chinese Nation

# CAI LUN'S IMPROVED PAPER

Before Cai Lun improved techniques for papermaking, writing used to be done either on wooden plates and bamboo slips, which were rather heavy, or on silk or cloth, which was too costly, or on hemp paper, which was too coarse.

Cai Lun, a eunuch of Emperor He Di, realized that the paper had to be of better quality as well as cheaper, if it was to be more widely used. He began his research by taking a small step to advance the current technology, which involved beating hemp fibers into a pulp, which was then pressed into thin sheets. He made a finer pulp, but the pulp was not fine enough. Furthermore, hemp, being the chief material for producing cloth, was too costly for papermaking. New materials had to be found.

In his search for a cheaper substitute for hemp that was still as fibrous, Cai Lun experimented with

≪ Ink brick. Over 1,800 years old, this ink brick still looks as good as new.

recycled cloth, broken fishnets and bark. He put these things into water to soak until they were washed clean. Then he pulped them in a stone mortar. The pulp was then pressed much the same way as hemp pulp was pressed. Paper made out of these materials was much cheaper, but not smooth enough. Cai Lun wanted to obtain a finer pulp so that the paper could be of better quality.

He tried putting in lime, hoping this corro-

Mural about trade caravans, Han Dynasty.

sive material would further break down the fibers of the cloth, fishnets and bark. The result was better than expected. Not only was the fiber more thoroughly broken, but the pulp was also whiter thanks to the blanching effect of lime. Cai Lun was excited at his discovery.

However, he found that the paper produced out of the blanched pulp still contained coarse fibers. Furthermore, the lime used during the pulping left small particles in the product. To eliminate these undesirable byproducts, Cai Lun thinned the pulp with water and put it in a wooden tub. He then sank a mesh into the water-pulp mixture for a while, so that the finer and lighter pulp settled evenly on the mesh. The layer of pulp was then dried, and became a sheet of paper that was white and smooth.

Emperor He Di (r. 89-105) was pleased with this new technique. He told Cai Lun to continue with his research and development toward mass production of the improved paper. Cai Lun was made a marquis for his ingenuity, and paper produced by the technique he developed came to be referred to as Marquis Cai Paper.

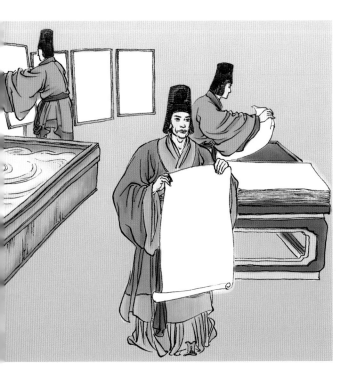

Papermaking process in the Eastern Han Dynasty.

# ZHANG HENG AND HIS EARTHQUAKE SENSOR

⌃ Zhang Heng's Earthquake Sensor (reproduction).

Zhang Heng (AD 78-139) was born in Xi'e, Nanyang Prefecture (in today's Henan Province). As a young man, Zhang Heng demonstrated an extraordinary quickness in learning, as well as an open mind. He was well versed in almost all types of ancient learning, but did not want to take for granted everything that the books told him. Instead, in AD 94, he left Xi'e to travel through the country to discover for himself how book knowledge fit into the real world.

In AD 111 Zhang Heng was assigned to a position in the government. Only having to perform mediocre routine tasks, Zhang Heng was able to focus his talents and research skills on astronomy after his office work was done. There were two current theories then concerning the nature of the universe. One of them involved a paradigm in which the heavens resembled an umbrella covering over the earth, like an overturned basin. The other drew a different image, and put a round earth at the center of the universe with all the other heavenly bodies moving around it in a celestial sphere. Scrutiny of both theories led Zhang Heng to believe that the second made more sense. He further developed the theory of a round earth at the center of the celestial sphere and made it the most widely accepted model of the universe.

When Emperor An Di heard about his wisdom in astronomy, in AD 115 he put him in charge of astronomical studies at the royal academy. In 117 Zhang Heng invented a hydro-powered model of an earth-centered universe.

A further great contribution Zhang Heng made to the history of science was what is believed to be the world's very first earthquake sensor that could register earthquakes and locate their origin.

The earthquake sensor was cast in bronze, in the shape of a barrel about 2.5 meters in diameter. Eight bronze dragons circled around the barrel, their heads aligned respectively to the east, south, west, north, northeast, northwest, southeast and southwest. Each of the dragons' mouths had a ball, which dropped into the yawning mouth of a bronze frog when an earthquake occurred, somewhere in the direction the dragon's head was aligned, so that people observing the machine knew where the seismic waves were originating from. This allowed ancient earthquake scientists to register earthquakes,

△ Zhang Heng invents the world's first earthquake-sensing machine.

as well as helping the government to locate the area of the quake so that relief could be delivered there.

Zhang Heng's earthquake sensor was put into use and proved reliable. In 138, for instance, when an earthquake shook the southeastern part of Gansu Province, the sensor, placed over 500 kilometers away in Luoyang, responded, and sent the dragon facing west to drop its ball into the corresponding frog. The researchers were skeptical because they themselves had felt nothing. Everybody was most surprised when reports of an earthquake came in from Gansu a few days later.

Zhang Heng was promoted for having built the earthquake sensor. Yet despite an increased oppor-tunities to be heard by Emperor Shun Di (r. 126-144), a Taoist worldview made Zhang see potential dangers in what was usually seen as success and favor; thus he shied away from such worldly temptations. However, his upwardly mobile career had already made the eunuchs jealous and desirous of removing him from the emperor's favor. As an old man, he asked the emperor, but without success, for permission to retire so that he could spend his remaining years in his hometown. In the end, Zhang Heng was not allowed to return home until after he died, and was buried in the land of his birth.

# HUA TUO THE MEDICINE MAN

⌃ Hua Tuo.

Hua Tuo was born in Qiao of the State of Pei (today's Boxian County, Anhui Province). He was very learned, and especially conversant in medicine. The government wanted to appoint him for his expertise, but he refused since he harbored a dislike for bureaucracy.

Instead, he chose to be an itinerant medicine man, and helped people with ailments. When he treated diseases, he identified what caused the body to malfunction and administered medicine accordingly, rather than just fighting the symptoms. He was also the first to perform incisions on the stomach, for which he was called the "Father of Surgery." He developed an anesthetic to go with major surgeries, 1,600 years before Europeans learned of anesthesia. When orally taken, it rendered the patient temporarily unconscious, considerably reducing the pain. He was also credited with inventing "Five-animal Boxing" exercises, what today would be considered aerobatic dances or yoga, which involved moving the patient's limbs, waist

and the other joints in a manner that drew from habitual movements of tigers, bears, deer, monkeys and birds.

After hearing of Hua Tuo and how miraculously he performed his healing, Cao Cao sent for him to treat his chronic headaches. Hua Tuo made his diagnosis and performed acupuncture. It worked wonders. Cao Cao was so pleased that he asked Hua Tuo to stay as his personal medical advisor. Hua Tuo did not want to accept the offer and tried to walk away. Cao Cao was so furious that he imprisoned Hua Tuo and eventually put him to death.

《 Gold inlaid bronze Boshan perfume burner of the Han Dynasty.

∨ Hua Tuo performing surgery. Legend has it that Guan Yu once had surgery done on his arm by Hua Tuo, without using anesthetic, for a deadly injury caused by a poison-tipped arrow.

# HOW CAO CAO BEGINS HIS POLITICAL CAREER

△ Cao Cao. He was given the posthumous title "Emperor Wu Di" of Wei. He was both a great strategist and a great poet.

Cao Cao was born in Qiao of the State of Pei (today's Boxian County, Anhui Province). While he was still a young man, he demonstrated his intelligence and talent. Cao Cao's political career began when he was commissioned as a military officer to fight the Yellow Scarf Rebels in Yingchuan. Military success soon elevated him to the position of chancellor to the prince of Jinan. He returned to Luoyang, the capital city, a few years later when the imperial government assigned him to a new post. When a scramble for power within the royal court created major confusion in the capital, a warlord named Dong Zhuo was sent for to clean up the mess. In reality Dong Zhuo was coming back to grab power. He offered Cao Cao a promotion in exchange for working with him. Cao Cao, whose political abilities were becoming better appreciated, declined the offer, seeing that Dong Zhuo's cruelty and folly as a politician would soon bring destruction down on him. Instead, Cao Cao stole out of the capital and traveled to Chenliu to join his father, who invested his entire fortune in his son's campaign against Dong Zhuo.

With a local tycoon and his cousin Cao Hong donating funds and personnel respectively, in addition to his father's support, Cao Cao built up an army of 5,000, which he put into training while he kept an eye on the political dynamics of a restive empire. Uprisings across the country had furnished local authorities with a perfect excuse to increase their weaponry. After Dong Zhuo had dethroned the emperor and killed him, then manipulated the coronation of another son from the royal family. Local governments all started to be roused in indignation, while at the same time secretly looking for possible

ways to slip into the power vacuum left by a weakened central government. Of all the local warlords standing up against Dong Zhuo, Yuan Shao was the greatest and most admired. Son of an eminent family, Yuan Shao was the governor of Bohai Prefecture when he built up his own army against Dong Zhuo, whom he had battled with while in the capital Luoyang.

In AD 190, anti-Dong Zhuo forces joined Cao Cao at Chenliu. The allies made Yuan Shao commander-in-chief and assembled an army of over 100,000. But, instead of launching a joint strike against Dong Zhuo, who upon hearing of the allied forces had abandoned Luoyang and moved the emperor to Chang'an, the warlords simply held their troops in wait. Cao Cao tried to talk his friends into further brave action: "I

△ Du Kang's Temple. Located in Ruyang, Henan Province, the temple is dedicated to Du Kang, the legendary winemaker, believed to be the first person ever to make wine. His name became synonymous with fine wines, as can be seen in one of Cao Cao's poems, in which he proclaimed: "*O! Du Kang, healer of all pain, and friend of sweet forgetfulness!*"

do not see what you are all waiting here for, when we are joined together in this war of justice against evil. Just think of what we have: Dong Zhuo has held hostage the emperor and burnt down the royal palace; the whole nation is outraged. Dong Zhuo is now doomed. We will fight him and defeat him, and we must do it now or never!"

His eloquence persuaded no one, because what he spoke of was not really what the allies wanted. Even allied commander Yuan Shao cared less about fighting Dong Zhuo than of cashing in on the current turbulence. Disappointed, Cao Cao marched alone, with his squad of 5,000, in pursuit of Dong Zhuo. Instead of waiting for Cao Cao to come and take up battle in Chenggao, Dong Zhuo sent his general Xu Rong to surprise him on his way at the Bianshui River. The ambush inflicted heavy losses on Cao Cao's troops. Back at the allied forces' camp, a frustrated Cao Cao saw his friends merely partying and forgetting about the war, until there was nothing left to sustain the joint campaign, and they each went back to where they had come from. Leaving these defeatists, Cao Cao rebuilt his army in Yangzhou. He was on his way to becoming a full fledged leader.

≪ Cao Cao the Great Statesman. His career as a great statesman began with his rising up against Dong Zhuo, and culminated when he became the virtual leader of northern China.

# THE BATTLE OF GUANDU

The war against Dong Zhuo ended disgracefully, and Cao Cao decided to work alone. He built up his troops again and, advised by his coterie, arranged for the royal family to settle on his lands, thus obtaining an edge in the fight for legitimacy from the fact that he, rather than any of the other competing warlords, was with the emperor. As his power grew and expanded, he came into confrontation with the domain of Yuan Shao, who was already powerful and dominant in northern China. Tensions built up and soon developed into a big clash in Guandu. It was a deadly wrestle for dominance between Yuan Shao the giant and Cao Cao the rising hero. One would have to go, and the winner would take all.

In AD 200 Yuan Shao took an army of 100,000 on an expedition to Xuchang, where Cao Cao had the emperor with him. Vanity about an apparent advantage led Yuan Shao into disheartening defeats, first in Baima (today's Huaxian County, Henan Province) and then in Yanjin (in today's Henan Province). Confident that he still outnumbered Cao Cao, he nevertheless had his troops cross the Yellow River to engage the enemy's main forces in Guandu (northeast of today's Zhongmu, Henan Province). Cao Cao was awaiting him there. A month passed without either of them gaining a decisive victory, until one of Yuan Shao's advisors, named Xu You, intercepted information that Cao Cao's troops had overextended their supply line.

Xu You suggested that Yuan Shao launch a surprise attack on Xuchang with a small unit, which could be maneuvered around Guandu. His advice was totally ignored by his commander, who believed he could easily crush Cao Cao's army. Before he could give further explanations, a courier from Yecheng, the base city, entered with a message accusing someone related to Xu You of wrongdoing. Shared blame by association placed Xu You on Yuan Shao's blacklist, and whatever else he said about the current campaign no longer mattered. Humiliated, Xu You deserted Yuan Shao's camp and surrendered to Cao Cao, an old friend of his.

Cao Cao was preparing to sleep, when he was told he had a visitor named Xu You. The news sent him into such a state of excitement that he could not wait to put his shoes back on, and ran out barefoot to meet his friend. Sitting in Cao Cao's living room, Xu You asked if Cao Cao had

a plan ready to stop Yuan Shao's advance, and how much food remained to sustain his army. Cao Cao gave him a deceptive answer, "Enough to last for another year."

Xu You snickered, "I do not think so."

"You cannot be fooled, can you? Yes, I only have enough food for six months."

Indignant over all the ambiguity, Xu You retorted: "Do you want to defeat Yuan Shao or what? Then you must be far more straightforward with me than you have been."

"One month," was the final and true answer, "after that, we will starve. So what do you think we can do?"

Xu You told his sly friend that Yuan Shao had his supplies and weaponry stored in Wuchao (today's Yanjin, Henan Province) but the place was badly guarded, and a small cavalry would be enough to raid it and burn all Yuan Shao's supplies so that his former lord could be crushed easily.

Cao Cao did exactly what Xu You told him. It was a thorough job and not a single grain was left for Yuan Shao. The fire at Wuchao sent Yuan Shao's forces into a panic. Some officers betrayed Yuan Shao, while those who did not were defeated in a campaign in which Yuan Shao lost his main force. He died two years afterwards. Another seven years passed before Cao Cao cleaned up northern China of all the pro-Yuan Shao forces, and brought it under his control.

---

> ⊙ Cao Cao Enforced the Military Law Strictly
>
> In the Battle of Guandu, Cao Cao issued the order "Soldiers who damage wheat will be punished to death" to protect crops. In his several tens of years of military administration life, he issued many orders to punish those who broke laws, committed breach of duty, or deserted in face of battles, and awarded those who made contributions. Moreover, he dealt out the income and production of his own fief to his generals, officials, veterans and the orphans and widows of the dead generals and soldiers.

《 The Guandu Battle. Cao Cao gains the edge by listening to Xu You and raiding Yuan Shao's granary.

# THREE REVERED VISITS

A descendant of the royal family of the Eastern Han Dynasty, Liu Bei entered the political arena of a troubled empire by volunteering as a military officer to fight the Yellow Scarf Rebels. His pursuit of power at first was not successful, and there were times when he had to work under Cao Cao, and then Yuan Shao. But Liu Bei left Yuan Shao after the Guandu campaign, and joined Liu Biao, governor of Jingzhou, who assigned him military and civil power over a township called Xinye. It was too small a place for Liu Bei's ambitions. While sighing over his muddled career, Liu Bei learnt from a gentleman named Sima Hui that just there in the countryside adjoining his township lived two wise men. Their sagacity as strategists was such that public opinion said, whoever engaged the counsel of either of them would be able to restore peace to the empire. Sima Hui told him that one of them was called Zhuge Liang, and the other was Pang Tong. As Liu Bei also learned from his advisor Xu Shu about Zhuge Liang as a renowned wise man, he finally decided he must visit him and try to get his help.

Zhuge Liang, like many of his contemporaries celebrated for their wisdom, had withdrawn from society, and lived in hermitage in Longzhong. It was a time of civil discord when the government had been weakened and warlords fought each other for dominance. Seeing no chance to put their wisdom to good use, and discouraged by the constant dangers of involvement in vain power games that were often likely to cost its players their lives, these hermits chose to distance themselves from too much social and political life, and retreated to the country, where they enjoyed the simplicity of rural life, though

《 Liu Bei paying Zhuge Liang a visit.

many of them awaited for their opportunity in the world to come.

Not wanting an interview he expected little from, Zhuge Liang hid himself from Liu Bei. Outside Zhuge Liang's house, Liu Bei and his two right-hand men, Guan Yu and Zhang Fei, waited for a long time but without success. He came a second time but again in vain. This of course upset Guan and Zhang. Liu Bei finally met Zhuge Liang when he came the third time. In Zhuge's secluded living room, Liu Bei confided in him.

Zhuge Liang's strategic viewpoint.

"This is a time of distress for the royal family, when crooked men have usurped power and disgraced the throne. It may be too big a task for a man of mediocre talent like myself, but I would really like to help to bring justice back to my country. I do not know how this could happen, and I beg for the honor of hearing whatever you have to tell me."

Touched by his sincerity and humility, Zhuge Liang explained to Liu Bei the current situation:

"Cao Cao has crushed Yuan Shao and his star is rising. Now he is in command of an army about a million strong. In addition, he has the emperor with him, thus acquiring the legitimacy his opponents do not have. This makes him formidable, and it would not be a good idea to meet him in a direct encounter. Sun Quan, on the other hand, has an unquestioned claim to Jiangdong (geopolitical term for Yangzhou, part of Anhui and Jiangsu, Jiangxi, Zhejiang, Fujian, eastern Hubei and southeastern Henan provinces), succeeding his father and older brother. He has the forbidding Yangtze River for his defense as well as the allegiance of his people. He would be a good friend, not someone you should try to attack.

"Now, Jingzhou (or Hanshou, a jurisdiction covering most of today's Hubei and Hunan provinces) being one of the most strategically important place, Governor Liu Biao will not be able to hold onto it for long. It could be like a gift for you, my lord, if you were interested. And Yizhou (or Chengdu, covering Sichuan, Yunnan and Guizhou provinces) is where there is the most productive soil. Its people are rich, but its governor Liu Zhang is stupid and very unpopular.

"But you, my lord, are a descendant of the royal family and people know you for your noble character. What I see for you is to take Jingzhou and Yizhou, befriend Sun Quan and build an effective government; so that, once opportunity reveals itself, one of your generals can launch a campaign from Jingzhou while you lead an army out of Yizhou, in a coordinated attack on Cao Cao. People will welcome you as their savior. And thus you would win, with the throne restored to its befitting dignity."

Liu Bei was so impressed by Zhuge Liang's strategic plan that he persuaded him to become his chief of staff.

# THE CHIBI CAMPAIGN

The victory in Guandu established Cao Cao's dominance in northern China. He now had a healthier economy to draw on, as well as a stronger army. Then he turned his eyes south, where Sun Quan and Liu Biao still stood in the way of his putting the whole country under one centralized authority.

In 208 Cao Cao advanced on Jingzhou. Governor Liu Biao had just died, passing his position to his second son Liu Cong. Liu Cong surrendered without putting up a fight, leaving Liu Bei no time to gather his forces in Xinye. With Cao Cao's troops advancing, Liu Bei had to retreat towards Jiangling, a city of strategic importance. But Cao Cao was faster. He caught up with Liu Bei at Changban (northeast of today's Dangyang, Hubei Province) and inflicted serious injuries on his troops. Before long Jiangling also fell to Cao Cao, and Liu Bei had to retreat to Xiakou (today's Wuhan), where he joined Liu Qi, Liu Biao's eldest son, and gathered a force of 20,000.

Cao Cao's advances made Sun Quan uneasy. When Liu Bei offered an alliance, Sun agreed. By the time the allied forces set up defenses in Chibi on the southern banks of the Yangtze, Cao Cao had camped his troops across the big river, ready for a major attack.

But there was one problem that was bothering Cao Cao. His soldiers, already exhausted from the hurried long march without rest, were now falling ill either because of the change in climate or seasickness on the battleships. To remedy the rocking of the ships, Cao Cao had them linked with chains and bridged their decks with boards so that soldiers could walk between them safely. What Cao Cao did not realize was that his solution to one problem only made his fleet vulnerable to another.

When allied commander Zhou Yu and Zhuge Liang noticed what Cao Cao had done to his ships, they decided to take advantage of the situation. First, they had to make Cao Cao believe that an officer named Huang Gai was about to surrender.

Cao Cao swallowed the bait. On the specified day, he waited for the signal that Huang Gai was deserting the allies to come to him. Suspecting nothing, he saw Huang Gai with his small fleet of loaded boats rowing towards them. On the boats Huang Gai had laid flammable materials, which were set on fire as soon as Cao Cao's fleet was close enough. The wind was just right for the allies, and before long Cao Cao's linked battleships were all aflame. When Cao Cao's soldiers saw the huge fire, which was illuminating the rocky cliffs, they panicked.

Meanwhile Zhou Yu's allied forces threw themselves ferociously at their enemy and destroyed them.

The Chibi campaign had a balancing effect on China's political dynamics, where Cao Cao's dominance was curbed, Sun Quan's position reinforced, and Liu Bei had finally obtained a foothold for further advancement.

⌄ The Chibi Campaign. Liu Bei and Sun Quan worked together against Cao Cao.

# SIMA ZHAO'S AMBITIONS

Ancient bronze warrior's head.

Decisive wars, especially those that had taken place in Guandu and Chibi, eventually cleared the political map of the Eastern Han Dynasty, leaving three dominant powers on it: Cao Cao, Liu Bei and Sun Quan. In 220 Cao Pi, Cao Cao's son, deposed the emperor and made himself Emperor of Wei. Liu Bei and Sun Quan quickly responded by proclaiming themselves emperors as well.

In AD 249 Sima Yi launched a coup in the Wei Kingdom and became its virtual leader. Although he died short afterwards, he passed state power onto his sons Sima Shi and Sima Zhao. Sima Zhao was ruthless when he became the prime minister. He killed off many people from the royal family.

By 260 Sima Shi had become so powerful that he openly disrespected the throne by wearing his sword while walking into the palace. Emperor Cao Mao (r. 254-260) was so intimidated that he rose up from his throne every time Sima Shi came to see him.

Court officials said to the emperor, "Great General Sima is held in great esteem and therefore should be given a dukedom." The emperor lowered his head, silent. Seeing this, Sima Zhao bellowed, "My father and we two brothers have made great contritution for the country. Can't I be a duke?" The emperor had to say, "How dare I am!"

The emperor did not dare to say no directly to his prime minister, but back in his private chambers he summoned his courtiers Wang Shen, Wang Jing and Wang Ye to remonstrate.

"Everybody knows what Sima Zhao is up to," said the enraged

emperor, "I would rather confront him and die than just sit here doing nothing."

He then produced his decree scribed on a piece of yellow silk that condemned Sima Zhao for treason, and declared: "What could be worse than that? I am determined. I am not afraid to die."

But Wang Shen and Wang Ye were fearful, and informed Sima Zhao of the emperor's decision.

Wild with anger, Emperor Cao Mao stormed out of his palace and marched to Sima Zhao's residence, bringing only a few hundred guards with him. Before he could do anything to Sima Zhao, he was killed by Cheng Ji, one of Sima Zhao's followers.

But when an emperor was killed, regardless of the circumstances, it was no small matter. In an attempt to escape responsibility, Sima Zhao pretended to be very sorry and blamed it on Cheng Ji, his instrument. He not only killed Cheng Ji but also his parents and wife and all their extended families. Then he made an emperor of Cao Huan, Cao Cao's grandson. The new emperor was a complete puppet. Sima Zhao had almost achieved his ambition to be emperor.

⌄ In contempt of the crown, Sima Zhao walks into the royal court with a sword.

# THE REUNIFICATION

The period of the Three Kingdoms (Wei, Shu and Wu) was approaching its end. In 263 Shu fell to the Wei, which in turn was replaced by the Jin, the dynasty of Sima Yan. Sima Yan was the son of Sima Zhao. As Emperor Wu Di of the Jin, or Western Jin (265-317), Sima Yan eventually ended the incessant state of civil discord that had torn China into warring states.

In AD 280 Emperor Wu Di of Jin appointed General Du Yu in command of an army over 200,000 strong for a campaign against Wu. To stop Du Yu's advance along the Yangtze River, the King of Wu, Sun Hao, laid barriers across the river with thick iron chains. He also had pointed devices submerged into the river to hit Du Yu's fleet.

When fleet commander Wang Rui learnt of Sun Hao's defenses across the Yangtze, he came up with a clever plan. He had his soldiers build dozens of wide rafts on which he placed straw men, dressed to resemble real soldiers, and sent some soldiers who were good swimmers to send these rafts downstream for the pointed obstacles to catch hold on them. Those good swimmers disposed of the rafts together with the obstacles, clearing the waterway. To overcome the dangerous chains, Wang Rui harnessed the power of fire. His soldiers built huge torches soaked in fuel, which they ignited when they came to each of the chains. The unrelenting flames melted down the iron so that the chains all sank to the bottom of the river. Wang Rui's fleet then captured many towns along the Yangtze.

Commander-in-chief Du Yu ensured that his army launched coordinated attacks from all fronts. While Wang Rui's fleet were advancing along the Yangtze River, his officer Zhou Zhi brought 800 soldiers across the river and approached Lexiang, a major military base of the Wu. Zhou Zhi had his soldiers wave many flags and torches on Bashan Mountain, giving the impression of a large army approaching. In the meantime, Wang Rui and Du Yu captured Wu's major cities Wuchang and Jiangling.

Du Yu decided to take advantage of his overwhelming success and march straight onto Jianye (today's Nanjing), the capital of Wu. His troops were unstoppable, crushing enemy defenses along their way.

Du Yu soon captured Moling (today's Jiangning, Jiangsu Province), the gateway to Jianye. The Wu commanders either died in the war or surrendered, leaving Sun Hao desperate for a plan. His courtier Hu Chong told him: "It is over, Your Majesty. When you cannot defeat them, I am afraid you can only join them."

When there did not appear to be any other way out, surrender seemed a good idea to Sun Hao, since he was still able to live on with all the luxuries he had become used to. His surrender marked the end of the old period of the Three Kingdoms, and the new reunification of China.

» Sun Hao's surrender.

# WAR OF THE EIGHT PRINCES

Emperor Wu Di of Jin died, passing the throne onto his mentally disabled son, who was to be known as Emperor Hui Di (r. 290-307). But the real sovereign was Hui Di's wife Jia, who ruled the empire ruthlessly for eight years. Not wanting to abdicate to Prince Sima Yu, a son whom the emperor had with an-

⌃ Table in the shape of a tiger biting an ox.

other woman, Empress Jia worked out a plan to have him eliminated.

Empress Jia had a letter dictated in the manner of the prince, urging the emperor to abdicate. Then she invited the prince to dinner and got him very inebriated. Semi-conscious, Prince Sima Yu yielded to the empress' manipulations and copied out her letter.

The next day Empress Jia had her husband summon all the officials and showed them the letter that the prince had copied out, accusing him of treason. The officials did not believe Prince Sima Yu to be capable of this, but when the empress compared the handwriting, they could hardly speak up for the prince. The case established, Empress Jia deprived Sima Yu of the title of crown prince.

Public opinion among court officials, always against

≪ Mural of a procession scene in ancient China.

⌃ Sima Lun captured Empress Jia.

soning as the pretext, Sima Lun sent Sima Jiong to arrest Empress Jia.

Dismayed, the empress demanded why he was here with all these armed officers.

"In the name of His Majesty, you are under arrest," was the answer.

"But my own words are in the name of His Majesty," cried out the empress, "I cannot consider any other decree as valid or effective!"

However, her words could not save her this time. She was arrested and beheaded.

Once he became the virtual dictator of the empire, Prince Sima Lun's ambitions grew. He went as far as placing the emperor under house arrest, and then ascended the throne himself. He rewarded each of his followers with a position in his government. When, given all the newly created positions, there was a shortage of marten tails, worn as a standard head ornament by the officials, the government improvised by using dog tails. Princes outside the capital learnt of the usurpation and soon joined in a fight for the throne. Because eight princes were involved, the war is referred to as the "War of Eight Princes."

Empress Jia and her tyranny, was outraged at the deprivation of Sima Yu's title. Prince Sima Lun saw this as a good opportunity to gain power. Worried about Sima Yu beating him to the sovereignty, he started a rumor that court officials were plotting his restoration. The rumor worked; fearful of retribution, Empress Jia had Sima Yu poisoned. Then, using the crime of poi-

# COALITION OF THE ROYAL FAMILY
# AND THE NOBILITY

In AD 316 the last emperor of the Western Jin Dynasty surrendered to other invading tribes. The following year, Sima Rui, a great-grandson of Sima Yi, restored the throne in Jianye (today's Nanjing). His dynasty was to be known as the Eastern Jin, and he became Emperor Yuan Di.

Sima Rui and his fugitive government were not highly thought of by the local nobilities of southern China. These were the interrelated big families that traced their ancestry to the Wu Kingdom in the Three Kingdoms period, and who had continued to prosper after the annexation of their state into the Western Jin. They were wealthy and looked down upon the northerners, calling them "rustics." Their contempt worried Wang Dao, a

gentleman from the north, for despite Sima Rui's arrival a month before none of these noble families had cared to pay him homage. Wang Dao discussed the situation with his cousin Wang Dun, trying to devise a plan to win over these southern nobilities.

The third day of the third lunar month was celebrated across southern China as a day when people went to the riverside to pray for good fortune and to cleanse themselves of any ills, so Wang Dao decided to arrange a big outing for Sima Rui when everybody would be out and would see him. On this festive day in 307, Sima Rui made an appearance in his elaborate carriage, parading past the celebrating crowds, followed by Wang Dao and Wang

《 Ancient rhinoceros-shaped wine vessel.

Sima Rui at his inspection tour.

Dun. The local people were very impressed, as were the noblemen. They changed their minds and extended the olive branch.

Next, Wang Dao reminded Sima Rui that he needed Gu Rong and He Dun, two of the most celebrated nobles, to join him in his government, so that the other big families would pay allegiance as well. On their part, the southern nobles were also starting to feel the need to enter into a coalition with the royal family from the north, with invading tribes from the north becoming a constant threat, while refugees pouring into the south were prone to riot. Seeing that a coalition would be in the interest of nobility from both the north and the south, Gu Rong and He Dun accepted the offer to join Sima Rui's government.

Because of the important role Wang Dao played in the founding of the Eastern Jin, many members of his extended family were given prominent positions in the government. So greatly did the royal family depend on the nobility, that people thought of the Wang family as sharing sovereignty with the Sima family.

# WANG XIZHI THE GREAT CALLIGRAPHER

⚊ Wang Xizhi.

The Eastern Jin Dynasty was the golden age for calligraphy, which had by then developed into a sophisticated art form. Wang Xizhi (321-379) was considered the greatest of all the calligraphers of the time.

Wang Xizhi had studied calligraphy with Wei Shuo from the time he was seven. He was a devoted learner, and within three years demonstrated impressive maturity for his age.

As he grew into adulthood, Wang Xizhi traveled widely to study different schools of calligraphy. He developed his own personal style as a calligrapher, combining elements of his precursors and coming up with his own creative aspects, which significantly differed from the archaic styles that had dominated the calligraphy of the Han and Wei periods.

He spent every minute of his waking hours thinking about calligraphy, and writing with his fingers on his own jacket — so much so that he wore out his

⚊ Wang Xizhi trading his calligrapher for geese.

≪ This stele with two characters meaning "Goose Pond" is at the entrance to Lan Ting garden. The two characters show the different styles of brush strokes, the second one being "fatter" than the first. Legend has it that Wang Xizhi had only been able to finish the first character, when a messenger came with an edict from the emperor; while he was with the messenger, his son Wang Xianzhi, also a calligrapher, did the second character for him.

As literature and as calligraphy, the "Prologue" to the *Lan Ting Collection* speaks perfectly of the spirit of the time in which it was created. The artistry of the brush strokes shows not only the well-trained touches of the author but also a sense of the emotional state of his being, which he invested in every stroke of his brush, and in the pattern in which all the strokes came together. It is a work of both scope and balance, so that the whole piece conveys felicity as well as a dynamic and beautiful rhythm. Ever since its creation, the "Prologue" has been valued as one of the greatest masterpieces of calligraphy. From it, Wang Xizhi acquired a timeless name.

≪ Wang Xizhi was so fond of geese that he traded his calligraphy for some from a Taoist practitioner. He kept these geese in a pond on Lushan Mountain and watched them all day and night. He had a "goose" engraved on the rock by a spring.

jacket where his fingers habitually marked their meditative movements. He practiced every day, and every time he finished, he would wash his writing brush in a pond in front of his house. As time passed, the pond turned so black, that people called it the "Ink Pond."

Wang Xizhi had a garden called "Lan Ting," near Kuaiji Mountain (Shaoxing, Zhejiang Province). It was a garden of comfort, elegance and simple beauty. In 353 Wang Xizhi and his friends had a get-together in Lan Ting. It was a nice day, full of easy talk and refined intellectual pleasures. Each of them composed verses to celebrate this occasion, which they put together into the *Lan Ting Collection*. Everybody agreed that Wang Xizhi should be the one to write a prologue for their collection. As if the Muses had planted the ideas into his mind, Wang Xizhi penned the prologue, which proved to be a masterpiece of literature and calligraphy, treasured and admired to this day.

### ⊙ The Own Calligraphy Style

Wang Xizhi liked to travel around the famous mountains and rivers. Whenever he saw the scripts of famous calligraphers, he would carefully imitate such scripts. It is said that when he was 53 years old, he still kept the habit of imitating the styles of ancient calligraphers. Once he went to bed, he still drew characters in the air with his fingers. Unconsciously, he moved the fingers on his wife's body. His wife was sulky and said, "Why do you always draw characters on other's body? Where is your own?" When Wang heard "your own," he suddenly realized that he should create a calligraphy style of his own. Later, he finally formed his unique style by concentrating others' merits.

# THE FEISHUI CAMPAIGN

The last few years of Emperor Hui Di (r. 290-307) witnessed the mounting internal discontent and resentment, leading to riots and insurrections that ultimately contributed to the fall of his dynasty. Meanwhile, nationalities beyond China's northwestern frontiers began to pour in, taking advantage of the social and political instability of the Han. In the 136 years from AD 304-439, states founded by these nationalities rose and fell in northern China and Sichuan. It was a period of much confusion, when different peoples intermingled and interacted, considerably altering the ethnological map of China. Historians refer to this period as the period of the "Sixteen States," after the sixteen most significant states of these ethnic groups.

The Qian Qin (351-394) was one of those states. In 382 King Fu Jian of Qian Qin subdued all other states in northern China and established his dominance. In 383 King Fu Jian, despite his officials' counsel against it, rallied his million-strong army for a campaign against the Eastern Jin, which had retreated south of the Yangtze River. His army and fleet advanced triumphantly. Within a

month, the pioneering troops arrived at the Huaihe River, standing by for an attack on Shouyang (today's Shouxian County, Anhui Province).

The good news from the front inflated Fu Jian's ego. Leaving his main force in Xiangcheng, he personally led a cavalry of 8,000 to Shouyang, anxious to destroy the Eastern Jin in a single battle.

Convinced the Eastern Jin was too weak to stand up against him, King Fu Jian dispatched an envoy through the front lines, with the view to calling on the enemy to surrender. But his envoy, named Zhu Xu, turned out to be an Eastern Jin commander who had been captured after surrender.

Although Zhu Xu had been made a senior official in King Fu Jian's court, he secretly maintained his allegiance to the Eastern Jin. Once again finding himself in the Eastern Jin camp, he felt the thrill of finally returning home, so he told commanders Xie Shi and Xie Xuan everything he knew about the Qian Qin Kingdom. He proposed that they attack first, before Fu Jian's troops all made it into battle position.

Xie Shi and Xie Xuan did as Zhu Xu advised. They gave Liu Lao the order to raid Luojian, which he captured. The bad news made Fu Jian rather uneasy. He walked up to the watchtower to observe his enemy.

What he saw sent terror into his heart: across the river, the Eastern Jin camps were lined up neatly, indicating a calm readiness. Farther away in the Bagong Mountains, what were actually phantasmal shadowy trees, to King Fu Jian, suddenly also looked like soldiers under cover. Disheartened, Fu Jian told his men to keep watch. Meanwhile, Xie Shi and Xie Xuan were anxious to cross the Feishui River to engage their enemy. They sent Fu Jian a letter challenging him to withdraw from the northern banks, so that there would be enough space for them to cross the river and launch a battle.

Fu Jian did not want to give his enemy any idea that he was afraid. Besides, it might be good for him to allow the Eastern Jin to cross the river, and then he himself attempted a surprise attack while

⌃ "We are victorious!"   This picture depicts what happened after the Feishui Campaign: Prime Minister Xie An was playing chess with his friends awaiting news from the battlefield, when a scout came running with the words "We are victorious!"

the enemy was halfway across.

At the agreed time, Fu Jian ordered his troops to fall back to clear enough room for his cavalry to launch a sudden attack on the Eastern Jin troops, who would be busy crossing the river. But things soon got out of control, after his soldiers, already fearful and sick of the war, broke into panicked, unstoppable flight.

Xie Xuan and his 8,000 cavalrymen quickly crossed the river and gave chase, completely destroyed King Fu Jian's army.

The battle at the Feishui River spelled doom for the Qian Qin. Fu Jian was killed by his officer, Yao Chang, in Luoyang, and his kingdom fell.

《 The Feishui Campaign.

# TAO YUANMING THE HERMIT

Tao Yuanming (365-427) received a Confucian education that highlighted social responsibility of the intellectual. But, the political system of his time being as it was, with accessibility to a successful political career determined by birth, he could find no proper position with the government to put his ideas to use; and so he eventually ended up as a hermit, taking delight in wine and simple country living.

Tao Yuanming.

There was not much a man educated in Confucianism could do other than to work with the government. Tao Yuanming found himself left with few choices but to take what was offered, to make a living, if not to fulfill his ideals as a statesman. His first government service started when he was 29. The vain, pompous bureaucratic life was utterly against his lively disposition, and he soon resigned.

He lived without employment for 11 years, before he entered the much-loathed bureaucracy for a second time. His second service lasted for just over a year, and ended in AD 401 when his mother died, an occasion for which it was customary as well as compulsory that a filial government official should resign and stay home for a long period of mourning.

He received government position for a third time. But nothing was to his liking, and he was torn between the perceived necessity to work and his love for freedom and simplicity in the countryside. After serving in some insignificant positions for less than

The picture depicts what Tao Yuanming versified in his *Home, I'm on My Way*: "Everyone is so happy that I am home. /Are those pines and chrysanthemums not awaiting my arrival? /And are those not the country roads we used to roam?"

> New Year's Painting, "Asking for the Way to Peach Valley." The fisherman is looking for a lost world.

80 days, he resigned again, this time for good. He could not even stay long enough to harvest the sticky rice he had grown for winemaking on the government estate. He turned into verse all the anxiety and distress he felt at being a magistrate, and the relief and happiness upon his ultimate decision to return to nature. *Home, I'm on My Way* became one of his masterpieces.

Living a secluded life, Tao Yuanming directed his mind to writing poems about country living, and how much he enjoyed it, despite (or maybe because of) its simplicity and hardship. With over 120 poems surviving to this day, Tao Yuanming is regarded as the initiator of a genre in Chinese poetry devoted to the praise of nature and country life, in authentic and simple language that became an attractive motif.

Shying away from the political realities of his time, Tao Yuanming envisaged what he believed was a perfect state of utopia in his epic poem, *Out of Peach Village*. It is a story about a fisherman stumbling upon a lost world, where he finds the inhabitants, who say they are descended from a community fleeing an ancient war, now living in a peaceful, righteous, paradisiacal society. There is no hunger, no poverty, no war, no crime, no laws, no government, and no tax collectors. Everybody lives happily according to their nature. Implying there might be nowhere to find or to found a society like this, Tao Yuanming had his fisherman leave the place, where a river flowed out into his world through a peach valley, and then lose his way back in his attempt to revisit it, despite all the markers he had left on his way out.

> Tao Yuanming coming from a wine party.

# THE LONGEST CANAL IN THE ANCIENT WORLD

The throne of the Eastern Jin Dynasty ended up in the hands of the usurper Liu Yu, who proclaimed himself emperor of the Song Dynasty. In the following one and a half centuries or so, sovereignty passed frequently from one dynasty to another, both in the south, from the Song to the Qi, then to the Liang, and the Chen; in the north from the Northern Wei to the Eastern Wei, then the Western Wei, the Northern Qi, to the Northern Zhou. In 581 Yang Jian took the throne from the Northern Zhou Dynasty and crowned himself as Emperor Wen Di of the Sui Dynasty. The capital was set in Chang'an. In 589 the Sui Dynasty conquered the Chen, putting China under one single sovereign again after 270 years of division.

The war-torn economy began to recover and prosper now that the "walls" between the south and the north were knocked down. People of different nationalities were able to interact and intermingle in a more peaceful way.

Yang Jian died in 604, passing the throne to his son Yang Guang, who was to be known as Emperor Yang Di (560-618). His empire was now economically stable enough for large architectural projects, and he wasted no time in starting them.

Emperor Yang Di first had a 2,000-kilometer-long ditch dug out from Longmen to Shangluo, forming a curved defense line for Chang'an the capital and Luoyang the eastern capital.

In the spring of 605, work on a new Luoyang, 9 kilometers west of the old city, began, together with the building of new palaces and royal gardens.

The most ambitious undertaking Emperor Yang Di launched was a great canal

> Emperor Yang Di's visit to Jiangdu. Wherever he went, the local economy was ruthlessly exploited, to make his trip a pleasant one, which led him to doom.

that ran some 2,400 kilometers from Zhuojun in the north, through Luoyang the eastern capital, to Yuhang in the south. Millions of laborers worked day and night for six years until this audacious architectural feat, equaling the Great Wall in its impressiveness, was completed.

By the Qing Dynasty, areas along the Canal had already become most prosperous, and were known as paradise.

The practicality of the canal was great. Instead of freight by road, food produced from southern China could be transported swiftly and on a large scale by canal — the only watercourse running north and south navigable by large cargo boats — to the north, the political and cultural center of the empire, where there was an imperative demand for food.

But, as such a colossal and costly project, the canal also became a heavy political liability.

In 612, despite his officials' counsel, Emperor Yang Di assembled an army of about 2 million strong,

Placing himself in command, and launched a great campaign against the Gaoli (northern Korean Peninsula). At Pyongyang, Emperor Yang Di laid siege to the city but could not capture it. His expedition was too far extended into the foreign land and his supply line failed, notwithstanding the 2 million workforce taking care of it. Seeing no hope to break into the city, the emperor ordered his men to retreat. The Gaoli army gave chase and crushed the Chinese forces, killing their commander-in-chief. Of the 300,000 frontier soldiers in the emperor's expedition, only 2,700 came back alive.

In 613 the emperor's second personally led campaign against Gaoli again ended fruitlessly. In 614 he prepared for a third one. After prolonged bitter warfare with success for either side nowhere in sight, the emperor agreed to make peace when the King of Gaoli offered to surrender. With a large percentage of the labor force recruited for the three consecutive campaigns, farmlands had been left untended, and the country's overall economy had weakened.

From 611 to 616, hungry peasants revolted, followed by landlords and military leaders who saw that the Sui Dynasty was doomed. In 617 the Governor of Taiyuan, Li Yuan, took Chang'an while Emperor Yang Di was away on a tour in the south. His royal guards were tired of their emperor's roving ways, and desired to return to Chang'an where their families were. The emperor felt desperate, knowing that his fate was sealed. He could not sleep unless his chambermaids patted him and comforted him like nursemaids do for small children. And when he did fall asleep, he slept with disturbed dreams and nightmares, which frequently woke him up.

In 618, taking advantage of the soldiers' discontent and homesickness, a general named Yuwen Huaji mutinied, and captured Emperor Yang Di. He had the emperor strangled to death. The emperor died believing himself to be innocent. He was given the posthumous title "Yang," which meant "indulgence in sensual pleasures and neglect of duty," a rather deserving comment on him as an emperor. Things for him seemed to have come around full circle, because that was the exact posthumous title he had given the last king of the Chen Dynasty, whom his father had conquered.

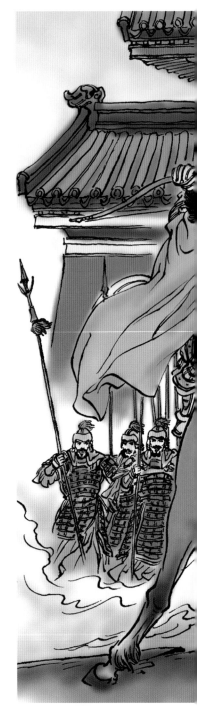

# COUP AT XUANWU GATE

In 618 Li Yuan proclaimed himself Emperor Gaozu of the Tang Dynasty (618-907). In 626, his second son Li Shimin killed Crown Prince Li Jiancheng and his younger brother Li Yuanji in a coup at Xuanwu, the north gate of the imperial palace. The coup ended in a forced transfer of sovereignty from Li Yuan to his son Li Shimin.

Li Yuan had four sons. Three of them survived into the Tang Dynasty. After Li Yuan ascended the throne, he named his oldest son Li Jiancheng as his heir, although his second son Li Shimin had proven to be wiser and more capable as a leader.

Since Li Shimin possessed wisdom and bravery, people gathered around him. This made Li Jiancheng jealous and insecure. Together with his youngest brother Li Yuanji, he spread damaging rumors about Li Shimin to their father, trying to malign him. Li Yuan believed what his sons said and Li Shimin fell out of his favor.

In 626, emergency border situations gave Li Jiancheng and Li Yuanji the excuse to propose that forces under Li Shimin's command be moved out of the capital city. On hearing this, Li Shimin decided to take pre-emptive action. He set up an elite squad for an ambush inside Xuanwu Gate. While passing through the gate on their way to the royal palace, Li Jiancheng and Li Yuanji suspected that something was amiss. Then Li Shiman suddenly appeared on a horse. Li Jiancheng tried to kill his brother with an arrow. But he was too frightened to pull open his bow. It was too late to escape either. Li Shimin shot Li Jiancheng with an arrow, while his warrior Yuchi Gong killed Li Yuanji. Li Shimin sent Yuchi Gong, spear in hand, into the palace, informing his father that Li Jiancheng and Li Yuanji had been plotting trea-

⊙ Scramble for the Throne

When the first emperor of the Tang Dynasty Li Yuan took the throne he conferred the Crown Prince on his first son Li Jiancheng. However, Li Jiancheng hadn't led army in any battles for the dynasty's establishment, whereas Li Shimin, the second son of Li Yuan, had fought battles himself and made many battle achievements. Therefore the conflict between them was inevitable. In the ninth year of the Yuande period (626) the battle between the brothers finally happened, that is the Coup at Xuanwu Gate.

The Mutiny at Xuanwu Gate.

son and had been killed. Emperor Gaozu was shocked when he learnt about the killing between his sons. His Prime Minister Xiao Deng told him he had to face the truth: "Li Jiancheng and Li Yuanji had not really deserved what you bestowed on them. They were the ones who had kindled and nurtured hatred between your sons. Everything shall be fine if you pass sovereignty on to Prince Li Shimin."

The old emperor knew there was little else for

him to do. He confirmed the offenses Li Shimin had charged his brothers with, and appointed Li Shimin, now his only surviving son, in command of all royal forces. Two months later, Li Yuan abdicated. Li Shimin was crowned as Emperor Taizong (r. 627-650). The period of his reign was known as Zhenguan.

# WEI ZHENG, A FREE-SPOKEN AND BRAVE OFFICIAL, REMONSTRATING WITH THE EMPEROR

Becoming a statesman during the early Tang Dynasty, Wei Zheng was born into a poor family in AD 580 in Qucheng, Weizhou (today's Daming County, Hebei Province). As a boy, he studied hard, and had a lofty aspiration. When he became an advisor to Li Jiancheng, he repeatedly reminded him that he had to eliminate Li Shimin.

After the coup at Xuanwu Gate, Li Shimin sent for Wei Zheng and asked him with a set face, "Why did you stir trouble between us brothers?"

"What a pity the Crown Prince had not listened to me. He need not have died," responded

⌃ Wei Zheng was always honest with Emperor Taizong.

⌃ Wei Zheng.

Wei Zheng, without losing his composure.

Despite his colleagues' anxieties, Emperor Taizong pardoned Wei Zheng for his honesty and talent and made him his advisor whose duty was to remonstrate with the emperor.

Wei Zheng possessed character and integrity. There are many stories about him being candid with the Emperor, while other officials had misgivings over telling him the truth.

Emperor Taizong once complained about his food. Wei Zheng told him: "Emperor Yang Di of Sui did not like his food either, and he complained a lot, until it became a reason his people did not like him. There is danger in caring too much about what you eat and Your Majesty is well advised to heed the warning. Content yourself with what you have, then you will find the food to be all very good; whereas, if you should be so disposed as to never feel satisfied by anything, then you will not enjoy any delicacy served onto your table."

"I would not possibly listen to such an admonition except from you," said the Emperor gratefully.

The Tang Dynasty reached a golden age during the reign of Emperor Taizong. While everybody else was busy lauding and glorifying the emperor, Wei Zheng submitted a memorial reminding him of the ten virtues he must be mindful of and practice amidst general plenty, which might otherwise foster pride and indolence. Emperor Taizong made a copy of this memorial and put it on a screen so that he could read it every time he looked up. "You let me know where I might fall short," he told Wei Zheng, "I shall work on all the flaws, otherwise I would be embarrassed to see you again."

Wei Zheng died in 643. Mourning over his loss, Emperor Taizong wrote the tombstone script for him. He recalled Wei Zheng as a friend who would always criticize him for any wrongdoing: "Polished bronze can be a mirror, it tells you if you have not dressed well; history can be a mirror, it tells you what is behind the rise and fall of dynasties; a man can be a mirror, a mirror of your soul, he tells you where you have gone wrong. Now that Wei Zheng is dead, I have lost my mirror."

⌃ Calligraphy by Wei Zheng.

# PRINCESS WENCHENG

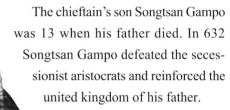

Tibet emerged from obscure origins to become an independent kingdom at around the same time that the Tang Dynasty was growing and prospering. The nation is believed to have originated from a land south of Gang-dis Mountain and the Yarlung Zangbo

⚑ Gilded Statue of Princess Wencheng in Tibet.

River. In 620 a chieftain established his rule over all the Tibetan tribes. But when he died in 629 from poisoning, two tribes seceded from the union.

The chieftain's son Songtsan Gampo was 13 when his father died. In 632 Songtsan Gampo defeated the secessionist aristocrats and reinforced the united kingdom of his father.

Songtsan Gampo moved his central government to Lhasa. As part of an open policy, he sent students to India. These students came back to develop the Tibetan language, based on Sanskrit and Khotanese.

The Tibetan king admired the culture of the Tang Dynasty. In 634 Tibetan envoys paid their first visit to Chang'an, to which Emperor Taizong of Tang responded by dispatching his envoys to Lhasa.

Songtsan Gampo sent his second delegation, this time to ask for the favor of marriage. Emperor Taizong agreed to marry him to a princess.

In 640 Songtsan Gampo sent his chancellor to Chang'an with 5,000 taels of gold and lots of jcwclry.

A young woman was chosen from the Tang royal family. She was styled as Princess Wencheng. The emperor had large quantities of marriage gifts packed for Princess Wencheng, including books on Chinese medicine, agricultural technology and craftsmanship, as well as tools and

« Tangka cloth painting of the story about Songtsan Gampo, the king of Tibet.

seeds. Maids, musicians and artisans accompanied the princess on her trip to Tibet.

Songtsan Gampo threw a great reception for his bride at the source of the Baihai River. He then built an elaborate palace in Lhasa for Princess Wencheng.

All the technical and cultural articles that Princess Wencheng had brought with her, along with the artisans skilled in various trades that Songtsan Gampo later requested and received from Emperor Gaozong, served as catalysts for the economic and cultural growth of Tibet.

Princess Wencheng died in Lhasa in 680. Over the 40 years she had lived in Tibet she greatly contributed to the development of this kingdom. She has been heralded as a symbol of peaceful exchanges between the Han and Tibetan peoples.

⩔ Princess Wencheng and Songtsan Gampo's wedding.

# XUAN ZANG THE PILGRIM

△ Xuan Zang.

A Buddhist monk in the early Tang Dynasty, Xuan Zang is primarily known for the pilgrimage he made to India, to bring back those Buddhist scriptures that China lacked for the proper study of Buddhism.

Xuan Zang started his journey in the fall of 627, together with two monks and a caravan of merchants. After they made it to Yumen Pass, Gansu, the two companions left him for fear of more perils ahead of them. Xuan Zang was caught trying to cross the border without proper papers. But the governor was so impressed by Xuan Zang's devotion when he discovered what his pilgrimage was all about, that

he helped him to pass through.

What was awaiting Xuan Zang was the vast expanse of the Gobi desert beyond Yumen Pass. It was a land forbidden to life, with scorching hot waves by day and the freezing winds blowing at night. Animals were barely to be seen, and still less, any signs of human habitation. Nothing but occasional trails of animal and human bones told of failed attempts to make the crossing, and warning of dangers still to come.

Not wavering, Xuan Zang walked for over half a month and traversed the desert, entering Gaochang (northwest of Turfan, Xinjiang). Leaving Gaochang, Xuan Zang walked for another year and finally arrived in India.

While in India, Xuan Zang spent years studying Buddhism in Nalanda Sangharama of Bihar, before he traveled elsewhere to talk with Buddhist masters. By the time he left India, he was already a celebrated Buddhist scholar.

In early 646, 18 years after he had started his journey, Xuan Zang returned to Chang'an with over 650 volumes of Buddhist scriptures he had selected. Monks and

≪ Dayan Pagoda. After returning from India, Xuan Zang was commissioned to translate the Buddhist scriptures. This pagoda housed the scriptures he had brought from India.

laymen alike all took to the streets to welcome his arrival. When Emperor Taizong learnt of his story in Luoyang, he sent his Prime Minister to bring him, so he could tell of what he had been through.

The emperor was interested in the mission that Xuan Zang had devoted himself to. He made arrangements for Xuan Zang to start to translate the scriptures he had brought back in a temple near Chang'an. Xuan Zang and his colleagues worked for 19 years and translated the Buddhist scriptures, 13 million characters long, into Chinese.

In 664 Xuan Zang died in the temple where he had worked. Besides the Buddhist scriptures that have survived in Chinese due to his commitment and devoted work, Xuan Zang coauthored *Nations to the West of the Tang Dynasty*. In this traveler's journal Xuan Zang told of the over one hundred states he had visited in the so-called Western Territory, and about the peoples and their lives. The book has been translated into many languages.

⩗ Nations to the West of the Tang Dynasty.

⩗ Xuan Zang on his pilgrimage.

# EMPRESS WU ZETIAN

Wu Zetian. Born in Shanxi, the only female monarch in Chinese history.

Wu Zetian was the only female monarch in Chinese history. She received a good education when she was a young girl, and grew up to possess remarkable wisdom and courage.

Wu Zetian became a maiden working in Emperor Taizong's study when she was 14. However, she then had a secret affair with the Crown Prince, the emperor's son, who often came to see his father, and had fallen in love with her.

After Emperor Taizong died, all the women in his palace who had not borne him a child had to become nuns. Wu Zetian was one of them. But the Crown Prince, now Emperor Gaozong (r. 650-683), having not forgotten her, brought her back into his palace. In 655 Emperor Gaozong dismissed the empress and married Wu Zetian.

Wu Zetian's coronation. While in the nun's temple, Wu Zetian persuaded the empress to help her. She then killed her own daughter and blamed the crime on the empress. The emperor, who disliked his wife because she could not bear him a son, divorced her and married Wu Zetian.

As empress, Wu Zetian began to help her husband with the administration, growing ever closer to the very center of the empire's decision-making process.

Emperor Gaozong died in 683, passing the throne to his son, Emperor Zhongzong, but mandating in his will that Empress Wu Zetian should be in charge of all major political and military affairs. Within two months, Wu Zetian deposed Emperor Zhong-zong for his alleged intent to pass the throne to his father-in-law, and crowned her younger son (Emperor Ruizong). Now she became the one pulling the strings, and all her opponents were eliminated.

The last step towards the summit of her pyramid of power was taken in 690. Wu Zetian ordered that her dynasty be called "Zhou," and her reign, "Tianshou" (Assigned by Heaven). She styled herself as the "Holy Empress," a title she ruled China with for 15 years.

The benefits she rendered the empire as a sovereign included some policies supporting farmers, especially tax reductions, tolerance towards criticism so that people offered their counsel without fear of punishment, strict laws against corruption, and an effective recruitment system that ensured those with talent were appointed into the government.

In 705 the prime minister and other senior officials coerced the empress on her deathbed to abdicate the throne in favor of Emperor Zhongzong, changing the name of the empire back to Tang. Wu Zetian died the same year. In her will, Wu Zetian

Wu Zetian at her coronation parade. Her courtiers all look in the same direction that she is looking.

The Blank Stele. Wu Zetian had this blank stele, 6.3m high and 1.49m thick, for her tomb, leaving herself to the mercy of the judgment of history.

gave up her title as monarch, wishing to be buried with her husband simply as his empress. She pardoned and spared from punishment the families of her husband's ex-wife and concubines, as well as those of the court officials she had made enemies with. Emperor Zhongzong resumed the throne. He approved her will and arranged her funeral according to her wishes.

It was a transfer of power in which no bloodshed was involved, with the sovereign plotted against quite willingly giving up her power and title, almost without parallel throughout Chinese history. As the only woman in China to ever scale up to the heights of power but also frankly own up to what she in reality was, while defying a highly male-centered culture, Wu Zetian was given a relatively deserved place in history, both for the duration of the Tang Dynasty as well as long afterwards.

# LI LONGJI AND THE KAIYUAN GLORY DAYS

Li Longji was born in 685 — an eventful period in the Tang-dynasty court. One year before his birth, his grandmother Wu Zetian, in collusion with Prime Minister Pei Yan, demoted his uncle Zhongzong to a lower title — the Prince of Luling; and his father, the Prince of Yu, was enthroned as Tang Emperor Ruizong. Ruizong, however, though a ruler at the prime of his life, remained secluded in another palace, and barred from the access to state affairs. Li Longji was made the Prince of Chu at the age of 3. When he was 6, Wu Zetian formally changed the name of the dynasty from "Tang" to "Zhou." Emperor Ruizong was reduced to the rank of "Crown Prince" and sent back to the palace designated to him. In the 12th month (Chinese lunar calendar) of the year 693, Li Longji

⌃ Li Longji, the Tang Emperor Xuanzong, had a good eye for people and appointed them properly.

Five Thousand Years of Chinese Nation

was made Prince of Linzi. That same year, his mother was framed by housemaid Tuan'er, and, on the 2nd of the 1st lunar month the following year, secretly executed in the palace, and buried to this day no one knows where. In the 8th month of the same year, his father was also falsely charged with "conspiracy."

⩙ Huaqing Pool. In the 10th lunar month every year, Tang Emperor Xuanzong, together with his favorite concubine Yang Yuhuan, would arrive to spend the winter. He handled state affairs and received his courtiers here, and would not return to Chang'an until the 2nd-4th month of the following year.

After the death of Wu Zetian, Emperor Zhongzong, inane and cowardly, left power to his wife Empress Wei and his daughter Princess Anle. Subjects who had made outstanding achievements for the country, like Zhang Jianzhi, were either demoted or exiled; the Crown Prince Li Chongjun was murdered; Wu Sansi and his ilk, who had been out of royal favor, staged a comeback; Empress Wei reinstated her own brother in power and urged her daughter Princess Anle to unscrupulously take bribes through awarding official ranks; she also ordered Taoist temples built at random and enslaved the people. State power fell completely into the clutches of the Wei-Wu clique.

In the 6th month of 710, after Empress Wei and her gang poisoned Emperor Zhongzong to death, Li Longji resolutely launched a palace coup and seized the whole Wei-Wu clique. Thus, Emperor Ruizong was restored to power. Li Longji, for his merits in stabilizing the state of affairs, was awarded the title, "Prince of Peace."

In the year 712, Emperor Ruizong, despite the objections of his daughter Princess Taiping, abdicated, and passed the throne to Li Longji. History refers to Li Longji as the Tang Dynasty's Emperor Xuanzong (712-756). On the 3rd day of the 7th month, Emperor Xuanzong led his palace guards to kill Princess Taiping's followers in a surprise attack. The princess fled in a panic into the South Hills. Later, she was ordered to kill herself. Emperor Ruizong, as father of the new monarch, now retired to the Hall of Happiness, and no longer had a hand in politics. It was only then that supreme power was transferred into the hands of Emperor Xuanzong. That year, he named his reign, "Kaiyuan."

It had only been through cut-throat struggle that Emperor Xuanzong had succeeded. But he still faced a tough situation after assuming power. Endless power struggles and upheavals had reduced the power of the central authority; earlier rampant corruption in appointing people had led to the swelling of officialdom. Yao Chong, promoted by the emperor himself, became the most prestigious Prime Minister of the time. Many of the measures, advanced by Yao, were adopted by the emperor, to lay the foundation for the Kaiyuan administration. Later, Song Jingji succeeded Yao as Prime Minister. He was also bent on elevating talent and made sure that officials were fit for their positions. Emperor Xuanzong was not only keen on selecting the top people, but on reforming management of officials at various levels and their rectification.

Tang Emperor Xuanzong, during the Kaiyuan reign (713-742), gave priority to economic development, for which a series of steps were taken, bringing about wide-ranging prosperity. During this period, owing to great efforts, both administrative and military, by the sovereign and his subjects, a comparatively clean and honest government took shape, ushering in the golden days of the Kaiyuan.

# AN-SHI REBELLION

Emperor Xuanzong, in his later years, began to lavishly shower favor on his concubine Yang Yuhuan, and conceded a considerable share of his power to Li Linfu and Yang Guozhong, two wicked officials. He himself indulged in sensuous pleasures while subsequently paying listless attention to the running of the state. Thus the Tang ruling class became more and more corrupt, bringing about the disastrous An-Shi Rebellion.

The An-Shi Rebellion refers to the treacherous war unleashed by An Lushan and Shi Siming. While Emperor Xuanzong was on the throne, ten garrisons were set up in important border regions to strengthen defense. The highest official of the garrison was called *Jiedushi*, entitled to both military command and decision-making in administration and finance, thus playing a crucial role. According to the usual practice of the time, a *Jiedushi* who had accomplished outstanding feats could be transferred to the court to assume the post of Prime Minister.

Li Linfu, while in power, not only tried to force civil officials out of the court, but also took a suspicious attitude towards the *Jiedushi* in the frontier areas, even framing them. At that time, some of the generals stationed in the border areas were *Hu* (a term used by the Han to refer to the non-Han nationalities in the northern and northwestern border regions). Li believed that the Hu were insufficiently educated, and should not be elevated to court office. But, in Emperor Xuanzong's presence, he suggested that more *Hu* should be appointed *Jiedushi*, and thus Xuanzong followed his counsel and did so.

An Lushan was part *Hu*. When young, he went into the service of Zhang Gui, *Jiedushi* of Youzhou (garrisoning the area around present-day Beijing). An was expert at currying favor with his superiors. Even Li Linfu, a man who paid lip-service only but always harbored ulterior motives, offered to put in a good word for An in front of Xuanzong. The emperor was taken in, believing An capable, and elevated him to the position of *Jiedushi* of Pinglu. Later, the emperor made him concurrently responsible for the garrisons of Fanyang and Hedong, as the *Jiedushi* of both areas, taking command of 180,000 troops, accounting for over one third of all the Tang border forces. But An Lushan, still not satisfied with his power and influence, left no stone unturned to win the emperor's affection and trust, who in turn granted An a dukedom, allowed his concubine Yang Yuhuan to adopt him as a godson, and gave him free access to the inner palace.

An Lushan, after wooing the emperor and Li Linfu to place trust in him, began to secretly expand the army. He elevated Shi Siming, Cai Xide and other valiant officers to key positions, appointing two Han officials Gao Shang and Yan Zhuang as his top advisors, se-

lected 8,000 warriors from soldiers of various ethnic groups in the border regions who had surrendered to him, and formed a crack force. They were storing up grain and fodder and preparing weaponry, anxiously awaiting the death of Emperor Xuanzong in order to stage a rebellion. On the 1st day of the 11th month, in 755, An Lushan rose up in Fanyang under the pretext of opposing Yang Guozhong, rallying over 150,000 troops, while professing to have over 200,000. An, together with his rebels, drove south, intending to fight their way into the Central Plains and then Chang'an, to overthrow the Tang Dynasty and to ascend the throne himself. During the Tianbao period (742-756), corruption in the court had sharply detracted from the combat effectiveness of its troops. Furthermore, the area was part of An's sphere of influence. Therefore, after the rebel forces had fought their way over, civil officials and military officers in the 24 counties north of the Yellow River fell into a great panic; some opened the city gate to usher in the rebels, many deserted the city, while others were captured and killed. The rebel forces met hardly any resistance and quickly swept over large stretches of land, bringing disastrous calamity upon the people, and wreaking havoc in the society. An's troops quickly captured Luoyang, an important city in the east, and swarmed towards the east gate to the capital Chang'an, Tongguan Pass. In Luoyang, An Lushan proclaimed himself "Emperor of Great Yan," appointing ministers, dispatching officials, and establishing an oppositional regime.

《 An-Shi Rebellion.

# JIANZHEN'S VOYAGE TO JAPAN

Jianzhen (688-763), with family name Chunyu, was from Yangzhou. During the Tang Dynasty, Buddhism was popular in Yangzhou, where crowds of monks collected from across the country and even from abroad, and Buddhist temples numbered over 30 to 40. Jianzhen's home also was bathed with a prevailing Buddhist aura. Under the influence of the family, at an early age, Jianzhen developed a strong interest in Buddhism. At the age of 14, with the approval of the Master Zhiman, he became a monk at the Dayun Temple. From then on, "Jianzhen" became his religious name. At the age of 45, disciples under him numbered over 40,000, as he had become an eminent disciple of Buddhism.

A statue of a seated Jianzhen, molded by Renji, one of his disciples, according to the monk's looks. The statue is still enshrined at the Tousyoudaiji Temple, and worshiped as a treasure of the country.

Among the Japanese envoys to the Tang court there were two monks, Rongrui and Puzhao. Entrusted by Buddhist circles in Japan, they came to Daming Temple in Yangzhou to pay a courtesy visit to Jianzhen, who was well versed in theory of the Buddhist precepts, and said to him: "It is about 180 years since Buddhism was introduced to Japan. However, we lack higher-status monks who are qualified to preside over ceremonies to ordain monks. For this, we intend to invite to Japan a learned, respected monk, to promote Buddhism and restore the disciplines." Jianzhen thus decided he would go in person. After four failed attempts to make the crossing, on the 27th day of the 6th lunar month, 748, he set out on a fifth voyage. The ship lost its bearings and drifted to Hainan Island, a long distance from Japan. After wandering around for a year, in 751 Jianzhen returned to Yangzhou. Tormented by the scorching heat of south China, on top of his years of suffering, he completely lost his eyesight. In 754, Jianzhen at the rather advanced age of 66, with a Japanese diplomatic corps, boarded a large ship bound for Japan. He eventually reached his destination and fulfilled his lifelong wish.

From 742 to 753, Jianzhen made 6 attempts to sail over to Japan, spanning over 12 years. In this period, more than 200 followers had wavered and deserted him, while 36 people had died during the voyage. Two people from the beginning persevered, following Jianzhen until his arrival in Japan; these were his disciples Situo, and a Japanese monk Puzhao. Both the Japanese government and the public were moved by Jianzhen's dedication, and prepared a grand and solemn ceremony in his honor. The Japanese emperor Syoumu then granted him the title Dai-sōzu, and placed him solely in charge of the preaching of Buddhist precepts. Jianzhen thus became the founder of the Risshū Buddhist doctrines on precepts in Japan. His lofty ideals, for whose fruition he had toiled for decades, were finally realized.

A welcome ceremony in honor of Jianzhen. Upon his arrival in Japan, Jianzhen was solemnly welcomed; later he became founder of the doctrines on Buddhist precepts in Japan.

Most of the Buddhist scriptures found in Japan had been handed down through word of mouth by monks, and were thus flawed, with many errors and omissions. Jianzhen, though blind, had an astonishing memory, and so was able to redress these deficiencies. Jianzhen, steeped also in Tiantai (or Tendai) doctrines, played an important role in their dissemination in Japan.

Jianzhen and his disciples also bequeathed a valuable heritage in architecture and sculpture. He had brought aboard the ship some figures of the Buddha. In Japan, he and his disciples, through the medium of dry paint (painted many times with lacquer over a mold, which is removed when the painting is completed), molded many such figures. Best known were the seated Buddha, Tathagata the

Apothecary, a 1,000-armed Mother Buddha, among others, found in the Hall of Gold at Tousyoudaiji Temple in Nara. Promoted by Jianzhen and his disciples, such sculpture techniques then were popularized in Japan. Jianzhen also brought along embroidered and painted portraits, copybooks of Chinese calligraphy, etc. Among these were authentic works by the calligrapher Wang Xizhi and his son Wang Xianzhi, both were great calligraphers of the Eastern Jin Dynasty. These later became standards for Japanese calligraphy and profoundly influenced this branch of the arts. It has been claimed that the inscription on the horizontal board hung in the Tousyoudaiji Temple was by the Empress Kouren in imitation of Wang Xizhi's style.

# LI BAI, "GOD OF POETRY"

Li Bai (701-762), styled Taibai, also named "Buddhist Lotus," was from Changlong, Mianzhou Prefec-ture, in central Sichuan (today's south of Jiangyou City, Sichuan Province). In the chronological history of Chinese literature, he was the second great poet, after Qu Yuan (339-278 BC), great patriotic poet from the state of Chu in China's Warring States period, Li was glorified by later generations as

△ Li Bai.

the "God of Poetry."

Li Bai, until he was 25 years old, lived in central Sichuan, reading and learning to fence, and living in seclusion and studying Taoism. He used to roam about Chengdu and Mount E'mei. In 742, Li Bai, at the age of 41, was on a tour of Yanxi, Huiji, when an edict from the emperor arrived, summoning him to the capital. To meet the emperor in the capital and to achieve his political ambitions had been Li Bai's dream for many years. Li Bai immedi-ately suspended his journey, packed and set out toward Chang'an.

The Tang Emperor Xuanzong soon beckoned

△ *Eight Immortals Drinking:* The "immortals" all lived during the Kaiyuan and Tianbao reigns of the Tang Dynasty; (from the left) Jiao Sui, Su Jin, Cui Zongzhi, Li Shi, Li Jin, Li Bai, He Zhizhang and Zhang Xu. As men of letters, they were all heavy drinkers, and unrestrained in their manners, hence the name.

Li Bai to his palace. He came under the spell of the young poet, so at ease and graceful in manner, and so eloquent and unrestrained in speech. The emperor himself was also talented and sociable, and found Li Bai much to his liking. A little while later, the emperor made Li Bai a *Hanlingongfeng*, a courtier who composed essays or poetry to entertain the sovereign and his high-ranking officials. One day, an anxious palace eunuch was delivering an urgent summon to the palace but found Li Bai so heavily intoxicated by drink, that nobody could wake him up. The desperate eunuch, in his haste, poured cold water onto the poet's head, doing his utmost to help him onto a horse and escort him to Xingqing

△ Illustration for the poem "To Wang Lun" (Wang Lun, a friend of Li Bai, bids Li farewell by the riverside). The poem reads: *Just before Li Bai sails, / stamping feet to Song of Farewell peals,/ For me, Peach Flower Pool so deep,/ to Wang Lun's sentiments cannot reach.*

Palace. At that time, Xuanzong and his favorite concubine Yang Yuhuan happened to be viewing peonies in full bloom. They stopped Li Bai and bade him to compose a few poems to enliven the atmosphere. With the expanse of flowers before his eyes, like masses of colorful clouds, Li Bai, fueled by wine and sudden inspiration, picked up a writing brush and wrote out in one sitting, the now famous "A Song of Pure Happiness." Xuanzong had the court musician Li Guinian strike up a tune, while he himself played the flute as accompaniment. But gradually, upon seeing the emperor shunning state affairs and addicted only to pleasure, while he himself seemed no more than a vehicle for their entertainment, Li Bai fell into an even deeper loneliness and gloom.

At that time, the emperor's favorite eunuch

Gao Lishi was quite influential. The Crown Prince had to address him as "Elder Brother," while the other princes, dukes and ministers called him, "Dad." Many high-ranking officials were promoted after fawning on him. Li Bai, however, thought this fellow rather beneath contempt. One day, the emperor fetched Li Bai to come and draft an edict. It so happened that Li Bai was also extremely drunk at the time. The eunuchs woke him up and supported him into the palace. No sooner had Li Bai taken his seat than he, in the emperor's presence, asked Gao to remove his boots for him. After being humiliated in such a manner, Gao was resolved not to take it lying down. Gao, hand in glove with Yang Yuhuan, whenever a chance presented itself, backstabbed Li Bai with criticisms in front of Xuanzong. Gradually, the emperor began to treat Li Bai coldly. Li Bai was obliged to leave Chang'an, and set out on another sightseeing tour.

Later the An-Shi Rebellion broke out, and Li Bai, at the age of 55, joined the staff of Li Lin, Prince of Yong, in an attempt to assist the prince in suppressing the rebellion. However, he had no idea that the Prince of Yong and Tang Emperor Suzong were not on good terms, and would soon fall out. On the excuse of "conspiring against the emperor," Suzong killed Li Lin, and also jailed Li

Bai on a charge of "following the conspirator." Fortunately, Guo Ziyi, an influential general, came to his rescue. Li Bai's life was thus spared, and he was exiled to Yelang (today's Tongzi, Guizhou Province). Feeling a strong sense of indignation at being clearly wronged, Li Bai went into exile, starting off on the last leg of his life journey. In 762 he fell ill in Dangtu, Anhui Province, and with his life in shambles, ultimately died in poverty.

⌄ Li Bai, intoxicated, holds Gao Lishi in contempt.

# DU FU, THE "POET SAGE"

△ Du Fu, aliea Zimei, self-styled "Shaolingyelao," usually addressed as Du Shaoling, was from Xiangyang (in present-day Hubei).

Du Fu (712-770) has enjoyed similar popularity to Li Bai; and the two are often ranked side by side in the history of Chinese poetry. Du Fu lived long enough to experience the decline of the Tang Dynasty, as it fell from its greatest heights. His poems mirrored the reality, people's misery, therefore, he was a great realistic poet.

Du Fu was precociously gifted. It was said that he had been able to compose poems from the age of 7. At age 14 to 15, he "came into contact with literary circles," socializing or exchanging works with men of letters. In 736, for the 1st time in his life, Du Fu took the imperial examination, with the hope of obtaining the academic title of *jinshi*[1] but failed. After that, he became contemptuous of the practice of vying for success in imperial examinations, and embarked on a journey of the plains lying across Shandong and Hebei provinces. At that time, his father happened to be the *Sima*[2] *of* Yanzhou Prefecture, and Du Fu spent between four and five "pleasant" years there, leaving us his earliest extant poems: "Ascending the Gate Tower of Yanzhou," "On a Painting of a Vulture," "A *Hu* Horse — to General Fang," among others. Of these, "Mountain Viewing" is the masterpiece, the final line becoming one of the

⩔ Illustration to the poem "Soldiers and Chariots upon Departure," depicting a soul-stirring scene of farewell, revealing the tragedy caused by the militarism of the Tang rulers.

best-known of all time: "*I resolve to climb up to the summit / when all the other peaks around look insignificant*" — revealing the extraordinary aspirations of the poet still in his teens.

Later on, Du Fu spent ten years in Chang'an, acquiring a deep understanding of the decadence of the ruling class and their ugly traits, as well as the hardships of the impoverished folk. His poems in this period include: "22 Lines to His Excellency Wei," "Soldiers and Chariots upon Departure," "Fair Ladies," "A Lyric of 500 Characters — Trip from the Capital to Fengxian County," and other masterpieces.

In the 11th month of 755, An Lushan rose in rebellion in Fanyang. In the 12th month, the rebels seized Luoyang; and in the 6th month of the following year, they stormed through Tongguan Pass. Emperor Xuanzong fled to Sichuan, and Chang'an fell. At that time, Du Fu and his family were on a journey up to Sanchuan from Fengxian (today's Pucheng, Shanxi Province). The Du family had just arrived in Fuzhou Prefecture (today's Fuxian, Shanxi Province), when news came that Tang Emperor Suzong had ascended the throne in Lingwu. Du Fu, after seeing his family properly settled, at once set off to serve Suzong, only to be captured by the rebels and driven back to Chang'an. In the 4th month of the year 757, Du Fu escaped to Fengxiang from Chang'an, to join Suzong's rallying forces. He was appointed by the emperor as *zuoshiyi*.[3] But soon Du offended the emperor by suggesting a pardon for Fang Guan, a prime minister out of favor; and at the beginning of the Qianyuan reign, Du Fu was demoted to the position of *sigongcanjun*[4] in Huazhou Prefecture. Because of incessant wars and famine, Du Fu was not able to support his family.

Moreover, he lost all hope in his future in officialdom. Therefore, in 759, he resigned from his post and went to settle down in central Sichuan, a land of peace and plenty at the time.

In the years following the An-Shi Rebellion, people found themselves caught in the depths of trials and tribulations. Du Fu himself also lived an unsettled life, barely able to scrape out a living. During this period, he wrote many poems, which were later immortalized, such as "Northern Expedition," "Jiangcun Village," as well as those commonly known as "Three Officers" and "Three Separations."[5]

In 765, Yan Wu, the *Jiedushi* garrisoning central Sichuan, died, and a series of riots erupted in the locality. Du Fu could no longer make a living in Chengdu, so he was forced to take his family onboard a small boat and begin the life of a wandering refugee. Perhaps, he originally intended to leave Sichuan, going eastward down the Yangtze River. However, hindered by illness and war, he and his family were halted halfway. At first he stayed in Yun'an for some time, and then lived in Kuizhou for nearly two years. At the age of 57, Du Fu finally sailed out of the Three Gorges, but was still forced to wander along the waterways of Hubei and Hunan provinces. Ultimately, on a passenger boat, Du Fu died prematurely at age 59.

In the last few years of his life, Du Fu reminisced about, or reflected on, his life as well as literary creations, and wrote long poems, which were in fact autobiographical accounts, such as "Travels in My Prime," "Travels in the Past," "Reflections," and " Reminiscences," as

≫ *Du Fu's Thatched-Roofed Hut* in Chengdu.  Du Fu's talents remained unrecognized all his life, as he roamed about, finally dying destitute. This is his residence in Chengdu.

≪ Illustration to the poem "Lament over the Hut Destroyed by Autumn Storm."  In the dilapidated hut, Du Fu lamented, "If only I had plenty of dwellings at my call / to shelter in comfort all homeless intellectuals!"

well as several short lyrics. For example, "On Meeting Li Guinian South of the Yangtze," the poet marveled at the bygone prosperity of the country, and lamented its present decline. In the few months before his death, he also wrote, "Turning the Boat Around," "Reaching Hanyang by Boat," "Returning to Qin in Late Autumn: Farewell to Colleagues in Hunan," among others. It was not until 43 years after his death that his grandson Du Siye escorted his coffin back to his hometown and final resting place, Yanshi, Henan Province.

---

[1] Academic title awarded to those who finished top in the national unified imperial examination.

[2] Assistant to the highest-ranking official of a prefecture.

[3] Court official rank, the main duties being of consultative nature.

[4] A staff officer keeping records of staff attendance, merits and demerits.

[5] Three Officers: "The Officer in Shihao," "The Officer in Xin'an," and "The Officer in Tong Pass."

Three Separations: "Separation from My Newly Married Husband," "Separation from My Aged Wife," and "Separation from My Ruined Home."

These six poems reflect people's grievances, and the sharp social contradictions of the time.

# HUANGCHAO UPRISING

⌃ Huang Chao (sculpture).

Towards the end of the Tang Dynasty, the court experienced increasing upheaval as a result of wars between local warlords, the usurpation of power by eunuchs, and sectarian strife among court officials. The year when Tang Emperor Yizong succeeded to the throne (859), a peasant uprising erupted in eastern Zhejiang; eight years later, a mutiny broke out in Guilin. Although both rebellions were suppressed by the court, antagonistic feelings among the common people rose higher and higher, and renewed uprisings grew larger and larger in scale.

In 875 Wang Xianzhi, a salt smuggler from Puzhou Prefecture (today's east Puxian County, Shandong Prefecture), together with the brothers Shang Jun and Shang Rang, led thousands of peasants in an uprising. Wang proclaimed himself to be "General of Justice and Heaven," "Commander-in-Chief of All Heroes." In the public bulletin, Wang sternly condemned court politics manipulated by wicked officials, as well as the heavy taxes and unjust awards and punishments. The rebel forces seized Caozhou (today's Caoxian County, Shandong Province) and Puzhou Prefecture, and their ranks swelled to tens of thousands. Then Huang Chao from Yuanju (northwest of today's Caoxian County), with his eight brothers, roused thousands of local peasants to take up arms in response. The two forces joined together, and an earth-shaking uprising was unleashed.

At the early stages, Wang Xianzhi was the supreme commander. The rebel forces adopted the strategy of roving warfare, and swept from (today's) southern Shandong to western Henan provinces, and then to eastern Hubei. Later, the peasant forces became divided after the two leaders had a disagreement. Wang Xianzhi and the Shang brothers led their troops in storming some prefectures and counties; he, however, asked the Tang commander-in-chief, seven times, to accept his terms of surrender, but was turned down. Eventually a telling blow was dealt to the rebels, killing tens of thousands of them, including Wang Xianzhi himself.

After Wang Xianzhi had met his doom, the peasant rebels again joined forces. They made Huang Chao their leader, calling him "General of Storms." At that time, government forces were powerful in the Central

Plains. When the peasant troops were about to launch an attack on Henan, the Tang court amassed troop contingents, to encircle and annihilate them. Huang Chao perceived the enemy's intent, and decided to direct his attack at the weak link in their defenses. He led his troops down south, successfully crossed the Yangtze River, fighting their way into eastern Zhejiang. They smashed all resistance along the way, and after a year's expedition, captured Guangzhou. After a period of rest and renewal in Guangzhou, they advanced northward. The Tang court's hastily summoned troops attempted to intercept them along the way, but were all crushed. In 884 Huang Chao and his 600,000 soldiers surged through Tongguan Pass.

The news that peasant troops had occupied Tongguan Pass struck terror into the hearts of those in the Tang court. Tang Emperor Xizong (r. 873-889) and the chief eunuch Tian Lingzi, together with the concubines, fled to Chengdu. The officials who could not manage to escape all walked out of the city walls to surrender. That same afternoon Huang Chao, riding in a golden sedan-chair, followed by his officers and soldiers, marched into Chang'an. People, both old and young, lined the streets to welcome him. Huang Chao's ascension ceremony took place in the Palace of Brightness in Chang'an, and his dynasty was named "Daqi." However, for a long time the peasant troops had been engaged in roving warfare, and stationed no troops in the places that came into their possession. Before long, Chang'an, formerly under their occupation, fell under attack by government troops. Zhu Wen, a general dispatched by Huang Chao for the defense of Tongzhou Prefecture (today's Dali, Shanxi Province), defected to the Tang court. Huang Chao was forced to retreat to Henan with the rebel forces and was besieged by Zhu Wen and Li Keyong. In 884 Huang Chao failed in his attack on Chenzhou Prefecture (today's Huaiyang, Henan Province). Pursued by government forces, he finally withdrew to Hulang Valley, where he met his heroic death.

≪ Towards the end of the Tang Dynasty, uprising peasants seized the Tongguan Pass, and led by Huang Chao, stormed into the city of Chang'an, where people, old and young, lined the streets to welcome them.

# DEPRIVED OF MILITARY COMMAND OVER A CUP OF WINE

⩓ Zhao Kuangyin, the Song Emperor Taizu.

In 907 Zhu Wen, through a series of coups, put an end to the Tang Dynasty, and established the Liang. In history this is referred to as the "Latter Liang," af-ter which the Tang, Jin, Han and Zhou, five dynasties altogether, were established in succession, spanning 53 years. This became known as the "Five Dynasties period." To distinguish them from previous dynasties with the same names, people call them the Latter Liang, Tang, Jin, Han and Zhou. Roughly coinciding with the five dynasties of the north, in southern China there arose the Former Shu, Wu, Min, Wuyue, Chu, South Han, South Pin, the Latter Shu

and South Tang, which, together with the North Han in the north, were called the "Ten States." Historically, this was the "Five Dynasties and Ten States period."

In 959 the Latter Zhou King Shizong, Chai Rong, died after an illness, and Chai Zongxun, at the age of only 7, succeeded to become King Gong of the Latter Zhou. Because the king was too young, there was restiveness in the state. In the following year, when the sovereign and his subjects were observing the Chinese New Year, word came that troops from Qidan[1] and North Han were driving south to jointly invade the Latter Zhou. Before discerning the truth of this information, the Chief Administrator Fan Zhi and other officials hastily sent Commander-in-chief Zhao Kuangyin and his troops north to block the enemy advance. At that time, Zhao Kuangyin was *Dianqiandujiandian,*[2] and concurrently *Jiedushi* of Songzhou Prefecture. He and Shi Shouxin, commander of the Royal Guards, were sworn brothers. Zhao, in control of military command, harbored the desire to become the sovereign.

After orders from the northern expedition, Zhao Kuangyin at once began military maneuvers, as if preparing to meet the enemy. When the troops moved into Chenqiao, a State Post (in today's Chenqiao Village, Fengqiu County, Henan Province), dusk was deepening, and they set up camp for

< Deprived of military command over a cup of wine.

the night. That night, on Zhao Kuangyin's prior instructions, Zhao Kuangyi (Zhao Kuangyin's brother), and Zhao Pu, a counselor, sent people into the camps, inciting mutiny to support Zhao Kuangyin as their new sovereign. There was a heated discussion among the soldiers: "The emperor is still too young to handle state affairs. Who will look after our interests if we risk our lives for the country? Better help General Zhao onto the throne before the northern expedition." Seeing the soldiers in action, Zhao Kuangyi and Zhao Pu immediately sent a messenger to ride to the capital, to make a secret appointment with Shi Shouxin and Wang Shenqi, two commanders of the Royal Guards, to say that Shi and Wang should act in coordination when Zhao returned to Bianliang. In Chenqiao, both officers and soldiers stayed awake all night, while Zhao Kuangyin pretended to take

Legend has it that during the Five Dynasty period, Chen Tuan, an immortal, lived in seclusion in the Wudang Mountains. He set up a fortune-telling stand at Kaifeng, foretelling Zhao Kuangyin's accession to the throne. After Zhao became emperor, Chen and Zhao staked Mount Hua on a *weiqi* game (Chinese chess, or Go), i.e., Chen would take the mountain if he won.

to bed after too much wine. At dawn Zhao Kuangyi, Zhao Pu and some other officers, burst in, weapons in hand, shouting: "We have no sovereign to rely on. We want His Excellency to be our sovereign!" While shouting, they crowded around Zhao Kuangyin, who kept pretending to yawn, and pulled the Dragon Robe[3] around him. Then all those present fell down on their knees and began to kowtow to Zhao, shouting in unison, "Your Majesty!" This is the historical anecdote "Dragon Robe of the Chenqiao Mutiny." That year, Zhao Kuangyin was 34 years old.

Zhao Kuangyin, now in the Dragon Robe, led his contingents of troops back to the capital and met no resistance along the way. The troops marched into Kaifeng. That very afternoon after their arrival, a solemn ceremony to hand over state power took place in the imperial palace. Zhao Kuangyin ascended the throne, proclaiming the establishment of Song, with Kaifeng as its capital, renaming it "East Capital." This became the Northern Song Dynasty (960-1127) of history.

After his ascension, Zhao Kuangyin, as Song Emperor Taizu, had no illusions of having no worries from then on. He knew he had to first stabilize the court, before he could divert his energy to end the chaotic state of affairs caused by disobedient warlords entrenched in different areas, so as to unify the country, and finally resist the state of Liao in the

north, which was growing more and more powerful.

One day he summoned his favorite subject, Zhao Pu, and asked him to deliberate on the causes for incessant wars and social calamities in the decades after the late Tang Dynasty. Zhao replied: "I believe the main reason lies in the fact that the local warlords are too powerful, causing a situation where the sovereign is weak while the subjects are strong. If we could reduce local warlord power, and claim back their military compliance, the country would become stable."

One day after this discussion, Song Emperor Taizu summoned Shi Shouxin, Wang Shenqi, Zhang Linduo, Zhao Yanhui and some other generals to a banquet. At the height of the drinking, the emperor suddenly called for a halt, and then bade all the servants to retire. After that he turned to his generals: "Running a country is a hard nut to crack; I was more at ease at the post of *Jiedushi*, and have never slept soundly since the ascension." Shi Shouxin and the others present could not all help wondering, "What else do you have in mind, Your Majesty?"

The emperor suddenly raised his voice: "Have you ever thought of the fact that everybody wants to be emperor? You have all pledged loyalty. Yet, once inferiors, in their desire for a better personal future, stage rebellion and force a dragon robe upon you, even if you are unwilling to act like that, are you sure that you can still retain control?" At this, Shi Shouxin and the others became most terrified. They could only keep begging the emperor to show them a way out.

The emperor sighed: "Life is short, and will flash by like lightning. Better to hand over military command, and work as a high-ranking civil official administering a district. Then, you can buy fertile land and luxurious houses, paving the way for happiness in posterity, living like fairies, drinking and enjoying comfort every day." The generals, hearing this, were full of gratitude, and thus retired. The following day, Shi Shouxin and others vied with each other to tender their resignations from office, on the excuse of ill health.

In this way the Song Emperor Taizu effortlessly disarmed his generals over a cup of wine. He eliminated the greatest threat to himself, by taking over military command from the generals, the very men who had pushed him onto the throne. By taking advantage of this favorable situation, he also snatched back, from the hands of the *Jiedushi*, military power, which from then on, whether central or local, was always in the emperor's grip. The influence of the *Jiedushi*, who used to lord it over the locals, gradually faded. The danger of the country being split by separatist regimes was thus eliminated.

[1] An extinct nomadic state, at that time situated north of China.

[2] Commander-in-chief of the Royal Guards.

[3] In China's feudal society, which lasted over 2,000 years, yellow was a special color for royal costumes; the emperor usually wore a yellow robe embroidered with dragons, which signified royalty.

# THE CHANYUAN AGREEMENT

In 988 Zhao Hen, the Song Emperor Zhenzong, succeeded to the throne, becoming the third emperor of the dynasty. During his reign, the situation along the northern borders grew more and more tense. Liao troops constantly invaded from the north, harassing and robbing the people, who, beyond all endurance, were crying out for help.

In 1004 the Liao once again amassed 200,000 troops. Under the command of the Liao Emperor Shengzong, along with his mother Empress Dowager Xiao, they set off from Youzhou and marched south to invade the Song. The Liao troops swiftly drew close to Chanzhou Prefecture (today's Puyang County, Henan Province) on the Yellow River, directly threatening the capital, Bianliang. Messages pleading for help flooded Bianliang. The panic-stricken emperor summoned his courtiers to work out a strategy. Someone immediately came up with the suggestion to move the capital elsewhere, which met with strong opposition from Kou Zhun, the Prime Minister. Kou Zhun had been awarded the position of Vice Prime Minister at the age of 31. However, being a man upright in his ways, he had offended Emperor Taizong. After a time he was demoted to a post in Dengzhou Prefecture (today's Dengxian County, Henan Province). In 1004, with the tensions in the border areas rising, Kou Zhun was appointed Prime Minister, in this time of emergency. Over the issue of Liao, Kou Zhun had always stood by the idea of resolute resistance. Displeased with the passive and concessionary attitude of the ministers, he advised Emperor Zhenzong: "Your Majesty, what we should do now is not move the capital, but work in concert to confront the challenge from Liao. If you take the field yourself, in command of the army, that will boost their morale and smash the enemy with one blow. Otherwise, how would we keep our territories intact, should the Liao troops fight their way over and storm into Bianliang, demoralizing our army?" After balancing the priorities, the emperor decided to act on Kou Zhun's proposal, and take command of the expedition himself. He also announced to his courtiers, "From today, no one is to talk of moving the capital in my presence."

The Song Emperor Zhenzong led his army to Weicheng (today's Huaxian County, Henan Province). The garrison forces were exhausted, after being caught in days of fierce fighting. The emperor's arrival greatly lifted their spirits. They beat off the Liao attacks, killing Xiao Dalan, an important figure in Liao, and frustrating the momentum of the enemy.

After passing on overall command to Kou Zhun, Zhenzong took up residence in a makeshift camp. The Song army scored a series of victories. The Liao troops, after besieging the town for days, simply could not break through, thus their spirits fell, and the attacks ceased. The situation began to turn favorable for the Song. At this moment, Kou Zhun believed that they should take the advantage and drive the Liao troops north, to expand on what they had achieved. However, Zhenzong wanted to play it safe and ordered his subordinates to negotiate a peace agreement with Liao. When Kou Zhun heard the news, he became so enraged, he almost fainted.

The peace agreement was signed in 1005, historically referred to as the "Chanyuan Agreement," as it was signed in Chanyuan. The Song Dynasty

Chanyuan Agreement.

was granted a fragile security at the cost of self-disgrace. After the agreement went into effect, Kou Zhun was dismissed from the post of Prime Minister. Emperor Zhenzong ordered troops stationed in the frontier areas to be reduced by large numbers, with no military preparations made along the borders. During the reign of Song Emperor Renzong, this appeasement policy continued; border defense was, to a great extent, neglected; much of the defense works became dilapidated from years of disrepair; the old weaponry was no longer suit-able for any meaningful offensive. In 1042 the Liao Emperor Xingzong deliberately spread word that he would send troops south, intending to exact greater annual tribute from the Song. The Song Emperor Yinzong did not dare to offend, hastily promising to yearly hand over 100,000 more bolts of silk and 100,000 more taels of silver. The Northern Song Dynasty once more had to swallow humiliation and plead for peace under the threat posed by the Liao. After that, for a long period, no major battles broke out between the two countries.

# FAN ZHONGYAN: THE PEOPLE'S WELL-BEING BEFORE ALL ELSE

Fan Zhongyan came from an impoverished family background. He enjoyed few familial joys in his childhood and hardly had enough food or decent shelter. He often took up lodging in Liquan Temple, working hard at his lessons, never resting for a moment. To lessen the burden on his family and to save time, every day he cooked a pot of rice gruel. When the food cooled down and hardened, he divided it equally into four with a knife, for two meals a day: two pieces for breakfast; and two for supper, plus salted vegetables to go with it.

In 1015 Fan was awarded the title of *Jinshi*, after leading in the imperial examination. Later he was appointed *Silicanjun*[1] in the Guangde Prefecture (today's Guangde, Anhui Province) embarking on a political career, which lasted over 40 years.

In 1021 Fan Zhongyan was sent to Taizhou Prefecture (now Taizhou City, Jiangsu Province) to work as Salt Administrator there. On taking up office, he at once went on an inspection tour of the sea walls and the local salt-making sites. The walls were dilapidated from years of disrepair. Not only had salt production been adversely affected, but farmlands and local houses had flooded whenever the sea waves had surged, leaving the locals to roam as refugees from famine. To address this, he submitted a report to his superiors, suggesting the construction of a long dyke along the sea coasts of Tongzhou, Taizhou, Chuzhou and Haizhou prefectures. After his proposal had been approved, in the autumn of 1024, Fan Zhongyan led tens of thousands of peasant laborers to the coast, undertaking a large-scale dyke project. Not long after, the project came to completion; and the dyke, wind-

ing its way across hundreds of *li*, ensured, from the havoc of the sea, production in salt fields as well as farmlands and houses. The grateful people felt so obliged to him, they named the dyke, the "Dyke of Fan."

Fan Zhongyan had a strong aversion against wicked people and wicked deeds, and was renowned for being candid and outspoken. During the ten years of his career as a court official, he was demoted and banished from the capital three times for telling the truth before the emperor, and offending influential interest groups in power.

In 1028 Fan Zhongyan was elevated to an official post responsible for the sorting and editing of the royal library collection, actually working as a royal literary servant. This position gave him an opportunity to gain easy access to the emperor himself as well as top court secrets. It was an admiring post. As long as Fan was obedient and tactful, promotion would not be difficult. Fan Zhongyan, however, preferred not to be "sophisticated." He raised opposition to the fact that, although Renzong was already 20 years of age, all decision-making power, whether political or military, still remained in the hands of Empress Dowager Liu. He appealed for the handover of state power from Liu to Renzong. Soon an edict was issued, expelling Fan Zhongyan from the capital and demoting him to the post of magistrate of Hezhong Prefecture (today's Yongji County, Shanxi Province).

Three years later, Empress Dowager Liu died. Emperor Renzong, cherishing the memory of Fan's loyalty and honesty, summoned him back to the capital and appointed him *Yousijian*, whose duty was to

△ Fan Zhongyan dredging Lake Tai.

make criticisms regarding court affairs. In 1033 the emperor was taken in by the slander against the empress, cooked up by Lu Yijian, the Prime Minister, and decided to depose her. Fan Zhongyan, however, was a man who called things by their correct names; and he appealed to the emperor to change his decision. As a result, he was again demoted to the post of magistrate of Muzhou Prefecture (next to today's Tonglu County, Zhejiang Province).

A few years later, Fan was transferred to become magistrate of Suzhou Prefecture. On account of his merit in hydraulic works, he was again summoned back to the capital, and elevated to the positions of *Daizhi*[2] of Tianzhangge and of magistrate of Kaifeng Prefecture. Lu Yiwei, the Prime Minister, was despotic in his methods, and practiced nepotism. Fan Zhongyan, in the presence of the

emperor, informed against Lu's practice of appointing people by favoritism. However, at that time Renzong had already placed all of his trust in Lu. Therefore, Fan Zhongyan was demoted a third time, and posted to Raozhou Prefecture as magistrate. In 1052 he died on the way to his new office in Yingzhou Prefecture.

_____

[1] An official in charge of lawsuits and trials.

[2] A high-ranking official at *Tianzhangge*, a subsidiary of *Hanlinyuan* (the Imperial Academy) mainly in charge of the collection of royal documents.

# WANG ANSHI'S REFORMS

Wang Anshi (1021-1086), styled Jiefu, literary name in later years being "Half Mountain," was from Linchuan (in today's Jiangxi Province). Wang was awarded the academic title of *Jinshi* in 1042, the 2nd year of the Kaiyuan reign. When Renzong and Yingzong were in power, he assumed a series of official ranks both at the local and central level, thus arriving at a deeper understanding of the so-cial realities, political flaws and crises faced by the country. Gradually a set of political and economic principles began to form in his mind. Once, in a proposal submitted to Emperor Renzong, he came up with ideas for implementing reforms.

After the death of Emperor Renzong, Yingzong

⩒ Wang Anshi's reforms.

was the country's sovereign for four years. Later, Zhao Xu, Song Emperor Shenzong, succeeded. The young emperor was ambitious and capable. Seeing the country was in decline, he was eager to smooth over the difficulties the court had encountered. In 1069 Shenzong had a one-to-one meeting with Wang Anshi, asking him for proposals regarding the running of the country. Wang answered confidently: "If the country is to be revived, the present habits should be discarded and new regulations and systems put into effect. "

In 1069 the Song Emperor Shenzong decided to press ahead with new laws in a comprehensive way. He appointed Wang Anshi as *Canzhengzhishi* (Vice Prime Minister), whose duty was to see that new laws were properly implemented; he also selected a number of young talented officials as Wang's assistants.

Wang Anshi's reforms mainly included the enactment of Crop-Cultivation Credit Law,[1] Corvee Law,[2] Farmland Rating and Regulated Tax Law,[3] Agro-Irrigation Law and Household Management Law.[4] The adoption of these laws consolidated state power, increased its revenue and lessened the people's burden, and thus enjoyed wide support among peasants, handicraft workers, small merchants and small and middle landlords. However, some aristocrats, bureaucrats and big landlords and merchants were dead set against the new laws, seeing them as an infringement against their vested interests.

Even Wang's learned, prominent friend Sima Guang also opposed his reforms, and over this the two friends fell out. Some princes and aristocrats slandered the new laws before Empress Dowager Cao, the emperor's grandmother, and Empress Dowager Gao, his mother. The two began to bear a grudge against Wang Anshi, and put pressure on Shenzong to abort the new laws.

In 1074 the Central Plains were hit by famine. Someone by the name of Zheng Xia painted a picture entitled *Refugees from Famine*. The painting was presented to Shenzong, who became very saddened at the sight of it. Some courtiers who were prejudiced against the reforms seized the opportunity, exclaiming in the presence of Shenzong, "The new laws have made a mess of the entire country!" The same year, Wang Anshi was dismissed from office and sent back to Jiangzhou Prefecture. In adverse circumstances, the new laws met with great obstacles in their implementation and were nearly abolished more than once.

In the 3rd month of 1085, Song Emperor Shenzong died, and the Crown Prince, Emperor Zhezong succeeded at the age of only 10. Empress Dowager Gao took over sovereign administration on his behalf. She appointed Sima Guang (1019-1086) as Prime Minister, and formally abolished the new laws. This evoked strong emotions in Wang Anshi's heart, and he passed away about a month later, at the age of 67.

---

[1] The law allowed poor peasants to obtain credit from the state, at relatively low interest, to buy seeds and other materials when the sowing season approached, and to pay off debts after the harvest, thus avoiding exploitation by loan sharks. This saved the broad masses of peasants from bankruptcy, and enhanced their initiative to engage in agro-production.

[2] The law stipulated that households of different incomes should pay different ratios of taxes in order to be exempt from corvee. This obliged the rich to pay more, and increased the state revenue.

[3] The law stipulated that farmlands across the country should be measured and rated by the authorities. Taxes should be levied according to the ratings of farmlands. This dealt a blow to the despotic gentry who had amassed large holdings of land but tried to evade taxes.

[4] The law stipulated that every 10 households should be grouped into a grassroots socio-military organization called "*bao*"; while a proper ratio of young males should serve as security guards in the slow season. The purpose was to maintain local security, to ensure against people staging rebellions, and to cut down the country's military expenditure.

# SIMA GUANG AND HIS
# ZI ZHI TONG JIAN

A glimpse of *Zi Zhi Tong Jian*.

Sima Guang, though conservative and against the reforms initiated by Wang Anshi, was an erudite recognized as a great scholar in history.

Sima Guang's father was strict about his early education, though the son was himself also a conscientious, hard worker. It was said that the child when only five or six years old was able to fluently recite *The Analects of Confucius* and *Mencius*. At age seven, he had already perused the *Zuo Zhuan*,[1] and could recount the essence of the book to adults. All this laid a solid foundation for his later accomplishments as a great scholar. Sima Guang in his teens was clever and quick-minded. Once, a group of children were enjoying a game of hide-and-seek in the garden, when one child fell into a huge water jar. At that time, household water jars were immense in size, and the drowning boy was struggling inside. All the other children looked on helplessly, crying loudly with fright. Sima Guang, who was reading inside the house, dashed outside. In that exact moment, his mind worked swiftly, and he picked up a huge rock and threw it at the jar. The jar broke and the water gushed out of the cracks. The child was thus saved.

When young Sima Guang was awarded the title of *Jinshi* and had started off on his official career, he took a strong interest in history and read a great deal, only to find that, despite the wealth of historical information left by various dynasties, there was still no book that had kept a complete record of historical facts from time immemorial to his day. Sima Guang decided to undertake the task himself. After Yingzong had fallen ill and died, Shenzong succeeded him; he thought highly of Sima Guang's work, in which he saw that exemplary rulers of some dynasties ran the country well and achieved prosperity; while other rulers ruined the country only to ultimately meet their doom. The emperor thought that the book could serve as a guide to rulers of later times. In 1084 *Zi Zhi Tong Jian* (*Historical Events Retold as a Mirror for Government*)[2], compiled by Sima Guang, was completed. By then he had a weak constitution and gray hair, and all his teeth falling out. *Zi Zhi Tong Jian* had consumed 19 years of the prime of his life.

He had been writing day and night, often forgetting to eat or sleep. To avoid oversleeping, Sima Guang made himself a round wooden pillow. While sleeping, whenever he turned over, the pillow, because of its round shape, would roll away and fall off the bed, and the thump would wake him up. Sima Guang called it a "pillow alarm."

Sima Guang possessed a sense of justice and of remaining faithful to reality. In *Zi Zhi Tong Jian*, his appraisals of monarchs of various dynasties, while affirming the good deeds they had performed

Sima Guang smashing the water jar.

for the country and people, also laid bare their exploitation and oppression of the people as well as their luxurious decadence, superstitions and absurdities. For people studying the history of China before the Song, this is of great reference value. The works are still an important cultural legacy left by ancient China.

[1] China's first chronological history covering the period from 772-464 BC, presumably written by the official historian of the state of Lu, Zuo Qiuming.

[2] A chronological account of historical events, for reference by later rulers in government.

# THE THREE SU: A FATHER AND TWO SONS

△ A statue of Su Shi in Meishan County, Sichuan Province.

During the Northern Song Dynasty, there lived a father and two sons who were all great men of letters renowned across the country. They were all ranked among the eight greatest masters of prose writing during the Tang and Song dynasties. They were the "Three Su": Su Xun, Su Shi and Su Zhe.

Su Xun, styled Mingyun, in his teens did not like to read, because he found the flowery, vain literary style of the time repulsive. His family and relatives were worried, telling his father: "Your son is shirking his lessons; why do you not interfere?" The father only smiled in response: "You do not understand him. I am not worried."

When Su Xun was 27, his first son Su Shi was born. Su Xun suddenly realized that, though he was a father now, he had accomplished nothing. Spurred on by the fact that his brothers and cousins had all excelled in the imperial examinations, he began to compel himself to study diligently. To master the

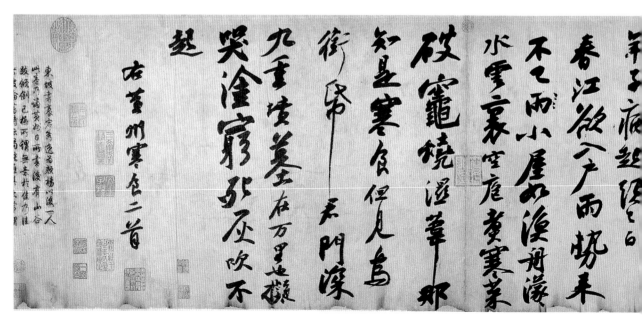

writing techniques of the ancients, he fired off hundreds of his own essays. After strenuous efforts, he became a master of prose writing in his time.

Three years after the birth of Su Shi, Su Zhe was born. Su Xun, late in his accomplishments, therefore placed all hopes of success on his sons. He gave them lessons himself, bidding them to recite and imitate works by famous writers, and revised and commented meticulously on whatever they wrote.

In 1056 Su Xun took his sons to the capital for the imperial examination. That year, Su Shi was 21, and Su Zhe, 18. The brothers effortlessly passed the examination for *Juren*,[1] and the examination sponsored by the Ministry of Rituals, as well as the Palace Hall Examination,[2] and were

⌃ The Three Su: a father and two sons.

≪ *Huang Zhou Han Shi Tie,* a poem and a work of calligraphy by Su Shi.

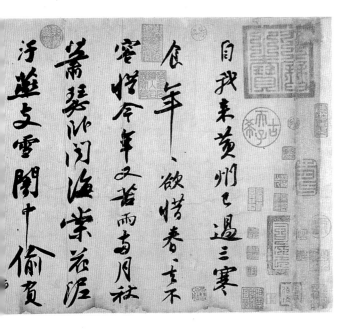

awarded the title of *Jinshi*. Witnessing his children launch into fame at such an early age, how could Su Xun not be overjoyed! But after second thoughts, he also grew resentful at the fact that he himself would remain in obscurity all his life. Hearing that Ouyang Xiu recognized people of talent, he sent, through a third person, over twenty essays written by himself, asking for enlightenment. Ouyang found he liked Su's writings. Well versed in phrasing, and unique in style, they

⊙ Su Shi (Dongpo) Cooked a Famous Dish

It is said that when Su Shi (Dongpo) was in charge of Hangzhou, he organized people to dredge up the West Lake and build a long bank around it to prevent the lands from drought and flood. These measures benefited the peasants around Hangzhou a lot, so they always presented him pigs as gifts. Su Shi (Dongpo) couldn't decline their kindness, so he ordered to cut the meat into large cuts, braise them, and sent a cut to every worker who dredged up the lake. The common people also learnt to cook this so-called "Dongpo Meat," and passed it down till today.

were really extraordinary. He then referred Su's works to Han Qi, the Prime Minister at the time, who also took a liking to them. Therefore, the court made an exception, and appointed Su Xun as *Jiaoshulang* at the Royal Secretariat. [3]

Thus, the father and the sons were simultaneously launched into fame in the capital, to be known as the "Three Su."

Of the three, Su Shi was the best accomplished in literature, and his literary feats were also the greatest of the Northern Song Dynasty. Ouyang Xiu had a high regard for Su Shi. He

once told his son: "Remember, in thirty years, people will forget me." What he said proved to be true. Ten years after Su Shi's death, just as Ouyang predicted, people were not talking about him but of Su Shi.

Su Zhe, Su Shi's brother, was also highly gifted. After the brothers had been both designated *Jinshi*, the Song Emperor Yinzong was so delighted that he said to the empress: "I have two talents for future prime ministers." Su Zhe was even more successful than his elder brother in his official career, eventually reaching the post of Prime Minister. His writings possessed both breadth and depth, making him well worth the name of a great master.

⌃ A string instrument invented by Su Shi.

[1] An academic title next to *Jinshi*, obtained through the imperial examination.

[2] The final round of the imperial examination, which usually took place in the palace hall, administered by the emperor himself. Those who came first were awarded as *Jinshi*.

[3] A central government organ in charge of royal document collection and also of a consultative nature, *Jiaoshulang* was a comparatively low official rank.

# SHEN KUO'S *MENG XI BI TAN*

⤒ Shen Kuo.

Shen Kuo (1031-1095) was from Qiantang (in today's Hangzhou, Zhejiang Province). He was a scientist of profound learning who possessed a wide range of knowledge. Shen Zhou, his father, was a low-ranking official below the county level, honest and upright in his ways. His mother Xu was a woman of fine cultural accomplishment. With such a family background, Shen Kuo had an admirable upbringing.

Shen Kuo, steeped in astronomy and calendars, once assumed the office of *Sitianjian*.[1] Shortly after Shen took office, his superior asked him: "Is the shape of the sun and the moon round or phased like a fan?" Shen Kuo had researched the problem long before and therefore answered readily: "Both are round like a ball. How do I know this? The evidence is in the waxing and waning of the moon. The moon has no light of its own. When the sun shines upon it, it reflects the light and also gleams. A crescent is formed because the sunlight only shines upon part of the moon, making it appear like a hook. When the moon is revolving around the earth and slowly moving farther from the sun, the sunlight reaches it at different angles, and the moon gradually appears rounder. Let us take a ball, for example. If we paint half of the ball and view it sideways, it looks like a hook; and if we look at it squarely, it looks round — from this we may determine the shape of the sun and the moon. "

As a historical figure who had lived ten centuries ago, it is truly remarkable that Shen Kuo described in such explicit terms, the shape of the sun

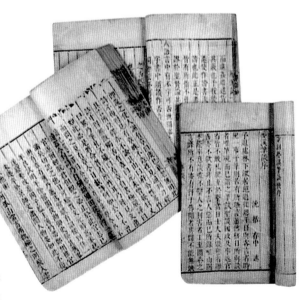

⤒ A glimpse of *Meng Xi Bi Tan*.

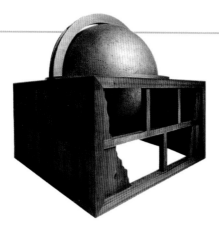

A celestial globe (model) used for State Meteorology during the Song Dynasty; such instruments had been made since the Han Dynasty.

orient a compass; he advanced the "layering" method for terrain survey; he was the first to introduce the scientific term 石油 (*shiyou*, petroleum), which remains in use until today; and he also came up with the idea to devise a yearly calendar based on the sun.

In his lifetime, Shen Kuo maintained a firm belief in science and an original and creative mind. His

and the moon, the source of moonlight, and the reasons for the waxing and waning of the moon.

Shen Kuo, in his twilight years, lived in seclusion. He had a garden built outside the seat of Renzhou Prefecture, naming it Meng Xi (Dream Brook). Shen lived there for eight years, not only fishing, boating, playing music and composing poems, but also spending his time reading and writing. He wrote down his experiences from his life and research in a book with academic themes, entitled *Meng Xi Bi Tan* (*Dream Brook Sketchbook*).

*Meng Xi Bi Tan* is rich in content. Apart from writings on the natural and social sciences, there are anecdotes in poetry and prose form, as well as fantastic stories. This work of encyclopedic caliber, consisting of 26 volumes, enjoyed great popularity. And later, *Meng Xi Bi Tan (Supplementary)* (3 volumes) and *Meng Xi Bi Tan (Continued)* (1 volume) were also published. The parts dealing with the natural sciences summarized ancient China's achievements in sciences, especially during the Song Dynasty, with a detailed record of the contributions made by laboring people in science and technology. For the first time in history it was pointed out, by Shen Kuo, that there existed declination in geomagnetic fields; he recorded a simple method of artificial magnetization, i.e., the creating of a compass by "rubbing a thin stick against magnetite;" he elaborated on four ways to

Shen Kuo working on *Meng Xi Bi Tan*.

works, apart from *Meng Xi Bi Tan*, include *Chang Xing Ji* (*Analects of Revival*), *Liang Fang* (*Precious Prescriptions*), and so on, totaling over 20 titles. *Chang Xing Ji* is an anthology of a comprehensive nature, containing Shen Kuo's important correspondence, reports, statements and tablet inscriptions, many of which relate to significant his-

toric events during the Northern Song Dynasty, making it a valuable source of historical information.

---

[1] An official in charge of meteorology and astronomy.

Five Thousand Years of Chinese Nation

# THE JINGKANG INCIDENT

Towards the end of the Northern Song Dynasty, in the state of Liao in northern China, under the rule of King Tianzuo (r. 1101-1121), the Nüzhen people (later called Manchu) in the northeast were cruelly oppressed and exploited, and yearned to cast off the yoke of the Liao. Aguda, taking advantage of his people's sentiments against oppression, in the process of attacking Liao, established the state of Jin, and after its founding continued to lead his troops against Liao.

In 1120 Song and Jin signed the "Agreement over the Sea," which meant the two countries simultaneously launched an attack upon Liao. After conquering the Liao, the land south of the Great Wall was to fall under the jurisdiction of the Song, while the Jin would be entitled to the Annual Monetary Tributes, which used to be the Liao's privilege. In reality, the agreement maintained the humiliation of the Northern Song. However, the Song Emperor Huizong approved it readily and did not guard himself against the Jin.

In 1122, only after seeing the Jin troops score a series of victories in their attacks upon the Liao, did the Song court send Tong Guan and Cai You to command 100,000 troops, to march towards the capital of Liao, only to be badly defeated. The Liao troops were no match for the Jin, but this time they encountered a rival whose combativeness was even weaker. Before long, the Song deployed 200,000 troops for another invasion of Liao, but again suffered a crushing defeat. To cover up his incom-

» The Jingkang Incident: The two weak and inept Northern Song emperors were taken prisoner by the Jin; this incident became known in history as the "Jingkang Humiliation."

>> *A Summer Day:* A poem and a work of calligraphy by Zhao Ji.

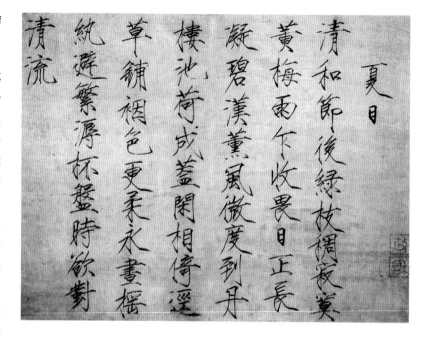

*A Summer Day:* A poem and a work of calligraphy by Zhao Ji.

petence and the defeats, Tong Guan conspired with the Jin to launch an attack on Yanjing, which was just what the Jin rulers wanted. For they had long harbored a plan to cross over the Great Wall, and seize more land. The Jin troops promptly drove towards Yanjing in three directions, and achieved this goal without hitch.

In 1125 the Jin King Taizong, after conquering the Liao, assembled his troops, and then drove south into the Northern Song. They advanced in two directions, seizing cities and military strongholds, crossing over the Yellow River successively, and pushing close to the capital (today's Kaifeng, Henan Province).

Previously, the Jin troops had once tried to fight their way into the capital. At that time, Song Emperor Huizong had fled south in panic, and conceded the throne to the Crown Prince, Emperor Qinzong. Faced with the initial attack of the Jin troops, the Song court managed to strike a deal by pleading for a humiliating peace. Once again the Song Emperor Qinzong still adhered to his old strategy of capitulation, and tried to plead for peace, rather than launch military preparations. This was conducive to the Jin's military strategy. At the end of 1126, the Jin troops surrounded the capital in a tight ring. At that time, there was still a garrison force of 70,000 inside the city. But Song Emperor Qinzong stubbornly harbored his illusions for peace. Instead of relying upon the army and civilians to put up a resistance, he foolishly entrusted defense to a band of street ruffians, the self-professed "Divine Army." As a result, the moment this useless band dashed out the gates, the Jin troops routed them, and seized the chance to ascend the tower gate of the city. The capital was thus very easily captured.

Even after the fall of the capital, the army and civilians still remained locked in fierce street fighting with the Jin troops, determined to fight to the last. But the inept Song

⊙ **Emperor Huizong of the Song Dynasty Created the Shoujin Style of Calligraphy**

Emperor Huizong, or Zhao Ji, was not only a painter, but also good at calligraphy. He created the unique shoujin style of calligraphy, featuring narrow and vigorous strokes, resembling leaves of bamboo and orchid. In fact this style is well-accompanied with his paintings. The so-called "shoujin" (literally lean gold) meant that his powerful calligraphy style worth gold. With its unique artistic feature, the shoujin style of calligraphy was imitated by the later people.

Emperor Qinzong sent messengers over to the Jin camp to plead for peace. The Jin commanders-in-chief Wanyan Zonghan and Wanyan Zongwang declared: "We have no intention of eliminating the Song. But before we withdraw, Emperor Qinzong must come in person to negotiate the terms of ceding territory." Qinzong indeed made a special trip to the Jin camp, together with several ministers, and presented his memorandum of surrender. He had intended to agree to any terms in exchange for the enemy's withdrawal. However, the Jin side, after accepting the memorandum, instead of pulling out their troops, on the contrary, put forward the demand that they had decided upon: to depose Emperor Qinzong and enthrone a new sovereign.

In the spring of 1127, the Jin troops held the Song emperors Huizong and Qinzong captive in the Jin camp. The Jin King Taizong ordered that Huizong and Qinzong be deposed. After that, Qinzong, Huizong, the empress dowager, empresses, imperial concubines, princesses, imperial sons-in-law, princes and ministers, totaling over 300 people, were thrown into prison wagons and delivered to the Jin as slaves. The Northern Song Dynasty, having survived for 153 years, perished as a result of the Jin invasion. This incident took place during the Jingkang reign of the Northern Song Dynasty, and is known historically as the "Jingkang Humiliation." The Song emperors Huizong and Qinzong have long since been scorned by later generations for being weak and abject.

» *Listening to Zither Performance* is one of the most delicate figure paintings passed down from the Northern Song Dynasty, colorful yet free of vulgarity. It was said to have been painted by Zhao Ji, Song Emperor Huizong. The composition is simple, giving a sense of the wondrous harmony of pines rustlings along with the musical notes.

# YUE FEI IN RESISTANCE AGAINST THE JIN

In 1127 the Northern Song Dynasty met its downfall. Zhao Gou, the ninth son of Huizong, known as the Song Emperor Gaozong, succeeded in Yingtian Prefecture (today's Shangqiu, Henan Province). That marked the beginning of the Southern Song Dynasty. Among the numerous heroes against the Jin that emerged in the Southern Song, Yue Fei was the most prominent.

Yue Fei was from Tangyin Prefecture (today's Tangyin, Henan Province). In the year he was born, the rivers had overflowed their banks due to torrential rains. A huge flood inundated his homeland, and his father was drowned. His mother managed to escape together with the baby, by riding in a water jar. Yue Fei's mother was a woman with fine qualities, adept at saving on food and clothing in order to pay for the son's education. Yue Fei worked hard at his lessons in his teens. He used to practice writing in the sand, since he could not afford paper. Later, he apprenticed himself to Zhou Tong, learning martial arts.

Yue Fei was wholeheartedly loyal to the country, never considering his own personal interests. The Song Emperor Gaozong once offered to build him a residence, but he graciously declined, saying, "There is still no peace throughout the land. In such a situation, how could I care only about my own family!" When asked how to achieve peace, he replied: "Only when civil officials are no longer greedy for money, and military officers, not afraid of death, will there be hope for peace in this land."

» Yue Fei in a battle against Jin Wushu.

In the 10<sup>th</sup> month of 1140, Jin tore up the agreement, assembled military forces, and put Jin Wushu in command, launching massive attacks upon the Southern Song in four directions. Emperor Gaozong, sensing a premonition of disaster, issued orders for the Song troops to resist. On the Emperor's orders, Yue Fei sent Niu Gao and Yang Zaixing, two generals under him, to confront the enemy. Then he ordered the volunteer forces in the Taihang Mountains to act in alliance, dealing blows to common enemies.

Before the operations, Yue Fei had a discussion with his staff about tactics. They came up with many ideas. Someone designed a new weapon, the long-handled hook-and-sickle. When the enemy charged toward them, the Song soldiers stepped aside to avert the charge, squatted down and thrust the hook-and-sickle forward to hook and cut the horse's legs. The wounded horses fell as did the Jin soldiers. Immediately, Song soldiers waiting in am-

bush rushed over and killed the soldiers on the ground. Jin Wuzhu, crestfallen, had to lead the remaining routed forces to a hasty retreat. Yue Fei led his men in tight pursuit, recovering quite a number of lost cities and towns. They fought their way until they reached the town of Zhuxianzhen, only 45 *li* (one *li* equals to half a kilometer) from the fallen capital.

As the news of the victories of the Song troops continued to come in, people on the northern banks of the Yellow River flocked to the army camp to extend their good wishes. Yue Fei was also greatly exhilarated. His eyes brimming with tears, he declared to the people: "We shall keep killing the enemy until we finally crush them in their own den — Huanglong Prefecture, and then I will drink heartily with you in celebration of the triumph!" Unfortunately, while Yue Fei, ambitious and confident, was making preparations for the northern expedition, Emperor Gaozong and Qin Hui, the treacherous Prime Minister, sent out 12 gold plates,[1] summoning him back from the front.

In the 7th month of 1141, *Youjianyidaifu*[2] Mo Qixie, instigated by Qin Hui, cast slurs on Yue Fei in his report to the emperor, blaming him for "benefiting from high rank and salary, growing conceited and arrogant, with waning ambition to accomplish feats, and a lack of determination to strive." In the 8th month that year, Yue Fei was removed from his position as *Shumifushi*,[3] and appointed *Wanshouguanshi*, a position of leisure without practical power. Then Qin Hui instigated Wang Jun, Vice *Dongzhi*[4] under Yue Fei, to falsely accuse Zhang Xian, Yue Fei's subordinate, of conspiracy for treason. In the 10th month of the year, the court made an announcement that Yue Fei and his son Yue Yun had been thrown into prison. In the 12th month, Zhao Gou issued an edict: "Yue Fei is to be granted a sentence of self-execution; Zhang Xian and Yue Yun are to be punished according to military law." On the same day, executive officials at *Dalisi*[5] passed the same verdict, and forced Yue Fei to sign a statement of confession. Yue Fei, who had been open and above-board all his life, wrote: "God is my witness! God is my witness!" Then he drank poisonous wine to end his life, at the age of 39.

### ⊙ Yue Fei's Mother Tattooed Characters on His Back

In the early Southern Song Dynasty, the peasant uprising led by Zhong Xiang and Yang Yao broke out in the Dongting Lake area of Hunan Province, who demanded "equality in social status and economy," and established the Dachu State. Legend has it that one day, someone knocked at the door of Yue Fei's home. It was Wang Zuo, a general of the Dongting uprising army. With generous gifts, he asked Yue Fei to join them. "I am a Song person when I live, and I am still a Song ghost even when I die." Yue Fei refused. His mother praised him for this and said: "I will tattoo '*jing zhong bao guo*' (loyal and contribute to the county) on your back with my best wishes that you will become a patriot hero." The stories that Yue Fei's mother tattooed characters on his back and that Yue Fei resisted against Jin's invading have been popular among common people for several hundred years.

« Portraits of the four patriotic generals of the Southern Song Dynasty. They are (from right to left): Liu Guangshi, Han Shizhong, Zhang Jun, Yue Fei.

⌄ A battering device — a weapon to ram into the city walls to pave the way for the infantry to storm into the city, used during the Song Dynasty to destroy the enemy's defense works.

[1] A token from the emperor for issuing orders to his officials and generals far from the capital, as confirmation of the urgency and authenticity of the order.

[2] A high-ranking official whose duty was to advise the emperor on important issues.

[3] A deputy position next to the chief of *Shumiyuan*, a key central government organ that controlled troop deployment.

[4] A rank of a military officer.

[5] The Supreme Court.

⌃ Mother Yue tattooing Chinese characters on Yue Fei's back. Mother Yue was patriotic; when Yue Fei was 18 years old, she herself tattooed four characters "*jing, zhong, bao, guo*" on Yue's back, to inspire him.

# WEN TIANXIANG, A MARTYR FOR HIS COUNTRY

Wen Tianxing (1236-1283) was born in Luling (today's Ji'an, Jiangxi Province) during the Southern Song Dynasty.

In the declining years of the Southern Song Dynasty, the court, entrenched south of the Yangtze River, had grown weak. In 1271 the Mongolians to the north put an end to their internal strife in a bid for the throne and established the Yuan Dynasty (1271-1368). They then turned their spearhead of attack on the Southern Song. In 1273 Boyan, the Prime Minister, with 200,000 troops at his command, seized Xiangpan. That served as a breakthrough allowing them to sail down the Yangtze River and, in less than two years, approach the suburbs of Lin'an, capital of the Southern Song Dynasty. Wherever the Tartars went, corpses of people they had slain were strewn across the field, blood stained the waters, farmland was laid waste, and economic activity came to a halt. This was a cruel, barbaric aggressive war unparalleled in history, and the Southern Song was being threatened with subjugation and genocide. Wen Tianxiang, who rose in such circumstances, became a great national hero against aggression.

In 1276 Yuan troops captured Lin'an (today's Hangzhou). After taking prisoner the Song Emperor Gongdi (r. 1275-1276), they swept south in an attempt to wipe out the remnants of the Song forces, and soon they stormed into Guangzhou. In the 8th month of 1278, the newly enthroned young emperor Zhao Bing conferred the aristocratic title of Lord Xinguo upon Prime Minister Wen Tianxiang. Towards the end of the year, Wen stationed his troops in Chaozhou (today's Guangdong Province), where he joined hands with Liu Zijun and other Song generals to encircle and annihilate a gang headed by ringleaders Chen Yi and Liu Xing. Liu Xing was killed, while Chen Yi, colluding with the Yuan troops, made an incursion into Chaozhou. Wen Tianxiang, however, moved to Haifeng (today's Guangdong Province) in time. Zhang Hongzheng, on the order of his brother Zhang Hongfan, the Yuan commander-in-chief, led troops in pursuit. Wen Tianxiang and his men were cook-

>> Wen Tianxiang in prison.

148

ing a meal at Wupoling, when the Yuan soldiers charged them. He was caught by the Yuan soldiers before he was able to fight back. Wen attempted suicide but failed. Liu Zijun, also caught, professed to be Wen Tianxiang, in the hope that Wen could seize the chance to escape. To his surprise, he had a showdown with Wen himself. Both claimed to be Wen Tianxiang. Finally the Yuan troops realized Liu Zijun was impersonating Wen Tianxiang and killed him. After that they took Wen Tianxiang to Chaozhou to meet Zhang Hongfan. Wen Tianxiang, in Zhang's presence, with his head held high, refused to kneel down. Zhang himself untied the rope around Wen, treating him as a guest. Wen Tianxiang asked to be put to death but this was refused. Then he was held in custody onboard the ship.

In the 10th month of 1279, Wen Tianxiang was taken to Yanjing. At first he was put up in an inn, where he sat up until morning every day. The Mongolians seeing that he would not bow, transferred him to *Bingmasi*,[1] watched over by soldiers. The Yuan Emperor Khublai felt sympathy for Wen

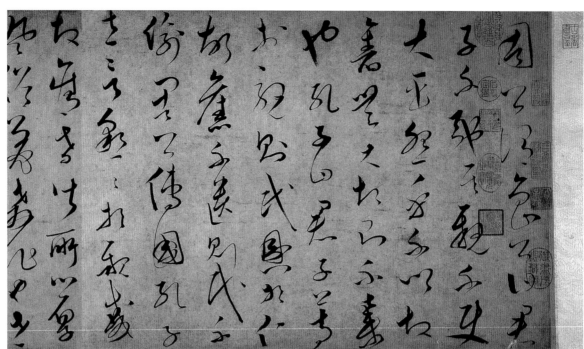

Detail from a work of calligraphy by Wen Tianxiang.

Tianxiang as a man of talent. He spared his life, only keeping him in custody.

Three years flashed by. The Yuan court sent people over, trying to persuade Wen Tianxiang to change sides. However, Wen did not waver in the slightest. In Zhongshan (today's Dingxian County, Hebei Province) someone professed to be the emperor of Song. He mobilized over 1,000 people and declared he would snatch Wen Tianxiang out of prison. In the capital, a man named Xue Baozhu wrote anonymously to Wen: "We have fixed a day for the uprising, honored Prime Minister. Please do not worry." In fear of an impending mass riot, the Yuan emperor summoned Wen Tianxiang, telling him, "If you are willing to swear loyalty to me as you had to the Song, I will make you prime minister." Wen Tianxiang replied, "I am the prime minister of the Song Dynasty. How could I surrender to Yuan? Please allow me to die!" The Yuan

emperor could not bear to have him killed, but people around him kept urging him on the necessity of Wen's death. Finally, the emperor issued an edict for Wen's execution, but soon regretted having made such a decision. However, it was too late by the time he sent people to stop the execution.

Wen Tianxiang was taken to the Firewood Market,[2] where tens of thousands of onlookers had already gathered. Before the execution, Wen Tianxiang remained calm and steady. He fell down on his knees, kowtowed twice towards the south[3] and then met his death heroically, at the age of only 47. The Yuan Emperor Shizu sighed: "A real man, yet he would not serve me. It was a pity to have him killed." Although Wen Tianxiang was killed, yet his imperishable line, "*Let my noble heart illuminate history*," and his moral integrity still remains an inspiration to people today.

---

[1] A government department in charge of social security, counterpart of modern-day police.

[2] Later named Caishikou, traditionally an execution ground in Beijing.

[3] Signifying his allegiance to the Song court, which was still entrenched in south China.

# EMPRESS DOWAGER OF GREAT LIAO

The Qidan were a branch of the northern nomadic tribes. They had lived along the Xilamulun and Laohahe rivers since the Northern Wei Dynasty (386-534). At the end of the 9th century, their various tribes grew in strength. In 907 Yelu Abaoji was made king of the Qidan, and later became the first emperor of the Liao. In 916 he was able to bring the tribal chiefs under his control, and abolished the tribal union system, proclaiming himself the Emperor of Heaven, and the founding of the state of Qidan, with Linhuang Prefecture as its capital. From then on, the country was alternatively referred to as "Qidan" and "Liao."

In the 2nd month of 969, the Liao Emperor Muzong (r. 951-969) was out hunting in Huaizhou Prefecture (in today's southeast Inner Mongolia). His entourage included Xiao Siwen, son of a cousin of the late Empress Dowager. During the hunt Muzong shot dead a bear, and his followers were exhilarated. Night had fallen and people were making merry around blazing bonfires. The Liao Emperor Muzong was crude by nature, and neglected state affairs; he cared for nothing but sleeping and drinking, and had thus aroused strong public indignation. That night, after Muzong had already fallen into a state of beast-like intoxication, and his bodyguards had also dropped their defenses, a

⌃ Fish-shaped jade used as personal ornament.

tragedy transpired: one of the bodyguards, who had a grudge against the emperor, assassinated him. Muzong had no offspring, meaning an impending crisis over the heir to the throne. In the dead of night, Xiao Siwen secretly sent a messenger back to the capital, informing Yelu Xian, the second son of the earlier Liao Emperor Shizong (r. 947-951), who lost no time hurrying to Huaizhou Prefecture the same night and thus ascended the throne as Emperor Jingzong, in front of Muzong's coffin. After that, the Liao Dynasty entered its heyday.

Liao Emperor Jingzong, who became a monarch overnight, made Xiao Siwen the Prince of Wei, as a reward for informing him of the crucial news. He also married Xiao's third daughter Xiao Yanyan, alternatively named Xiao Chuo. Jingzong had suffered ill health ever since childhood, and for a long time was not restored to health. The clever, beautiful and understanding Xiao Yanyan demonstrated consideration toward her husband in a variety of ways. While discussing state affairs, she often made amazing comments, displaying her political and military caliber. Jingzong, who was bedridden all year round, often offered her opportunities to handle political affairs.

In 982 Jingzong died of illness. His 12-year-old eldest son Yelu Longxu was made

Ornamental headdress made of gold and silver, worn by the female members of the Liao royal family.

Campaign, and recover the 16 prefectures of You and Yun. In the 3<sup>rd</sup> month of 986, he dispatched armies, via three routes, for an invasion of Liao. Xiao Yanyan, in face of the advancing Song armies, remained calm in counterattacking and wise in military maneuvers. The Song troops were again crushed, sustaining heavy losses both financially and in terms of lives.

Xiao Yanyan was clever. After the triumph, she remained coolheaded in assessing the situation, and gave timely support to the Western Xia bordering on Song to the northwest. Thus the Western Xia began to pose a threat on the northwestern borders of the Song. An alliance between the Liao and the Western Xia directed against the Song began to take shape.

At the same time, Xiao Yanyan also waged war against the nomadic tribes to the west, and Korea to the east, forcing them to swear fealty to her. The Song were sandwiched between two enemies, and had to take defensive action. Xiao Yanyan, however, continued to send troops south, who looted and often returned in triumph. In 1004 the Liao Emperor Shengzong and Empress Dowager Xiao, taking command of 200,000 troops, swept south, approaching Chanzhou Prefecture, only to be tightly surrounded by hundreds of thousands of soldiers and civilians of the Song. They were obliged to sign the "Chanyuan Agreement," an agreement well known in history. Thus a political situation with the Liao and Song in antagonism began to form.

In the 12<sup>th</sup> month of 1009, Empress Dowager Xiao handed state power back to Shengzong. She died of a serious illness at the age of 57.

Emperor Shengzong. State power was in the hands of Xiao Yanyan, now revered as "Empress Dowager Enthroned by Heaven." The widowed dowager and her son, on the one hand, had to face the Song, who could invade any minute; while, on the other hand, they had to be on the alert for noblemen coveting the throne now taken by the young emperor. Threatened with potential crises all around, Empress Dowager exhibited no signs of panic but instead masterminded events "behind the curtains." She made an analysis of the situation and gave priority to military power. She employed various means to cultivate good relations with the generals. Yelu Xiezhen and Han De, two powerful men in the army, became her top aides.

Zhao Kuangyi, Song Emperor Taizong (r. 976-995), believed that Liao now had "an immature emperor and the country was unstable." He wanted to avenge the Gaolianghe (or Youzhou)

Gold belt, Liao Dynasty.

⌃ Empress Dowager Xiao.

# LI YUANHAO FOUNDING THE WEST XIA

⌃ A Western Xia grand copper seal, each side measuring 4 centimeters; the characters in the Western Xia language, carved in relief, with relatively wide edges.

During the Song Dynasty, in northwestern China there emerged a feudal secessionist power called the West Xia (1038-1227), founded by an ethnic group known as Dangxiang, a powerful adversary of Song.

During the early Song Dynasty, political strife among the Dangxiang aristocrats led to a war. One of the aristocrats named Li Jipeng defected to Song. In the middle of this situation, the Song Emperor Taizong wanted to eliminate the secessionist regime, so he ordered Li to move his family to the capital (today's Kaifeng, Henan Province). However, Li Jiqian, Li Jipeng's brother in his 20s, was unwilling to move. He summoned the members of the clan, saying: "We are here our own masters. Once in the Song capital, our lives would be at others' disposal. What should we do?" Li Jichong, Li Jiqian's brother, said, "Why not kill the Song envoys while they are distracted?"

Li Jiqian had a follower who he had always taken into his confidence, named Zhang Pu, a Han. After a moment's reflection, he said, "Now every tribe has adopted a wait-and-see policy. The Song troops are stationed nearby, only a day's trip from here. We cannot stand idle while the army comes. Better retreat to the north of the desert and make settlements there, and then liaise with other tribes

and plan to stage a comeback."

In 983 Li Jiqian launched several offensives against the Song troops but, lacking in strength, was defeated each time, with even his mother and wife being taken prisoner.

In 1004 Li Jiqian was slain by an arrow during a battle with Tibetans. His son Li Deming took his place. Li Deming, however, petitioned the Liao for an aristocratic title, while also pledging the loyalty of a subject to the Song. As a result, both the Song and Liao made him the "Western Prince of Peace." Li Deming lived in peace with the two countries and expanded trade ties with them, thus boosting socio-economic development among the Dangxiang.

The Dangxiang people grew more and more influential, inspiring in Li Deming a desire to proclaim himself emperor and establish a state. He moved from Xiping Prefecture to the town of Huaiyuan (today's Yinchuan, Ningxia Hui Autonomous Region) and renamed it Xingzhou Prefecture, making it the capital. Copying the Song system, he made his son the crown prince, but he died of illness before his accession.

During the reigns of Li Jiqian and Li Deming, influenced by the Han feudal economy and culture, the Dangxiang were in a transition period from late clanship to feudal society, with ripening conditions for the establishment of a state.

In 1031 Li Yuanhao, son of Li Deming, inherited his position. He was expert at martial arts and versed in the laws and military strategies of Song, as well as knowing painting. Li Yuanhao was determined to found his country in accordance with the feudal system of the Han.

In 1038 Li Yuanhao proclaimed himself emperor of the country of Great Xia with Qingxing Prefecture as the capital. This local regime controlled present-day Gansu, Ningxia, Qinghai, Shanxi and parts of Inner Mongolia. Lying to the northwest of Song, it is historically referred to as "West Xia."

Li Yuanhao emulated the Song in establishing an official system. Then he ordered that the country's written language be formulated in imitation of Han characters. This writing system was in use throughout the nearly 200 years of the West Xia and even for a long time after, playing an important role in the political, economic and cultural development of China's northwestern region.

A warrior in Western Xia (color woodcut). The warrior is in red battledress, looking dashing and awe-inspiring; his colorful costume provides important insight into the Western Xia's military affairs and culture.

Li Yuanhao, the Xia Emperor Jingzong, adept at both calligraphy and painting.

# WANYAN AGUDA, NÜZHEN CHIEFTAIN

The Nüzhen people from long ago lived in northeast China, boasting a long history. From the 10th century, most of them lived in various tribes dotted over a large expanse of land under the rule of the Qidan. In the mid-11th century, Liao was on the decline, while the Nüzhen tribes were on the rise; especially the tribe of Wanyan, led by Wugulun, annexed others and expanded outward,

forming a formidable tribal league.

In the 2nd month of 1112, in Changchun Prefecture (today's Zhaoyuan County, Heilongjiang Province) on the Huntong River, the willows were turning green and everything was full of life. Luxurious, elegant tents were put up, of which the

⋙ Aguda at the banquet.

tallest and grandest was surrounded with soldiers, heavily guarded. That was where the Liao Emperor Tianzuo Yelu Yanxi had taken up residence.

Inhabitants from the surrounding areas had been forced to flee afar. People knew that the Liao emperor had arrived once again to hunt and fish. A luxurious "Banquet of Fish" would follow large-scale fishing. Civil officials and military officers and chieftains of the vassal Nüzhen tribes would come to pay courtesy calls to the emperor and offer their congratulations.

In the royal tent, the "Banquet of Fish" had been arranged, and the chieftains of the Nüzhen tribes were ushered in to take their seats. The Liao emperor, inflated with pride as he received congratulations from the Nüzhen chieftains, was looking around and discovered that Wanyan Wuyasu from the Wanyan tribe was missing. Somebody told him that Wuyasu was seriously ill and had sent his younger brother Wanyan Aguda over on his behalf.

A gold cup. Unearthed from a Jin-dynasty underground cellar, carved with baoxiang (an imaginary flower design consisting of petals, buds and leaves, popular in ancient Buddhist tradition) flower patterns.

When the drinking was at its height, Liao Emperor Tianzuo, in high spirits, ordered the Nüzhen chieftains to dance in turn. When it came to Aguda's turn, he rose and replied coldly, "Sorry, I cannot dance." The emperor took up his cup and drank it empty, saying, "The Nüzhen are all good riders and archers and enjoy dancing and singing. Why do you say that you cannot dance?" Though Emperor Tianzuo pressed him, Aguda remained motionless as he stood, as if his eyes were glistening with flashing swords, shining with hatred. The emperor felt a bit shaken. To ease the tension and embarrassment, another Nüzhen chieftain offered to dance. The banquet continued. When it came to an end, people moodily dispersed.

Aguda's obstinacy and disobedience made Emperor Tianzuo sense that something was weighing on his mind. He regarded Aguda as someone dangerous.

The following day, he called in a minister, Xiao Fengxian and said, "At yesterday's banquet, Aguda appeared arrogant and disrespectful. This is no common fellow. We should find an excuse to eliminate him, otherwise he will pose a threat in the future."

Xiao Fengxian, after thinking a while, said, "Aguda is rude by nature. He refused to dance at the banquet because he is ignorant of etiquette. If we were to kill him on a thin excuse, that would make the Nüzhen hostile to us. Even if Aguda were really plotting something, what is there to be afraid of, since they are nothing but a small tribe?" Hearing this, Emperor Tianzuo once more felt relieved.

In 1114 Aguda and troops he had called from various tribes, numbering over 3,500, were assembled by the Lalin River and taking an oath. After praying to the heavens and the earth, they condemned all the crimes of the Liao. Aguda announced, "All the troops should do their utmost. For those who perform feats: slaves and servants shall be granted freedom; civilians, awarded official ranks; and officials, receive promotions according to their merits. Should anyone dare to break the oath, off with his head and with those of his family!"

The Nüzhen troops marched into Liao and won the first battle. They then continued their advance. In the 10th month of that year, Aguda seized Jiangning Town. The Liao troops' morale lowered, and they were routed several times. Aguda's ranks gradually swelled.

In 1115 the chieftain Aguda, with the support of the country's aristocracy, ascended to the throne of emperor. "Liao" means "iron" and Aguda thought that iron, though hard, easily rusted away. Therefore he named his dynasty "Jin" (Gold) and made Huining Prefecture (south of today's Ahcheng, Heilongjiang Province) the capital. Aguda became the Jin Emperor Taizu. After that the Jin became the biggest threat to the Liao.

# GENGHIS KHAN UNIFIES MONGOLIA

⌃ An arrow-satchel used by the Mongolian cavalry.

In 1162 Ke'elun, wife of Yegaisu, chieftain of the Qiyan tribe in Mongolia, gave birth to a boy. That day, Yegaisu led his men in pursuit of the Tartars. He successfully captured two Tartars. One of the captives was named Temujin. To commemorate the victory, Yegaisu also named the newborn baby, Temujin.

Because of the incessant military conflicts between the Tartars and the Mongolians, Temujin spent his boyhood in battle. When he was nine, Yegaisu wanted to find a girl to be his future wife, so he took him to a relative of his mother. On the way, Yegaisu met Dexuechan from the Wengjila tribe. When the latter learned of his intent, he engaged his daughter Bi'ertie to Temujin.

On the way home, Yegaisu met with a group of Tartars at a banquet. According to custom on the grasslands, he dismounted from his horse and sat down at the banquet. The Tartars recognized Yegaisu, their foe. They covertly put poison into his meal. Yegaisu died not long after returning home.

Temujin resolved to carry on his father's mission. He knew too well that only with the support of certain tribal chieftains could he strengthen himself and defeat the enemy. Therefore he gave a black ermine overcoat, a part of his wife's dowry, which he held precious, to Tuowolilehan of the Kelie tribe and addressed him as "godfather." Then he swore brotherhood with Zhamuhe, chieftain from the Zhadala'er tribe. They joined forces and defeated their common enemy, and snatched back Temujin's wife.

The victory made Temujin grow in power. Many of his former subordinates and warriors gradually joined him again. In 1189 a number of chieftains unanimously supported him as their Khan (title of the supreme ruler of ancient nomadic nationalities).

In 1201 Temujin defeated Zhamuhe. In the following year he wiped out the remnants of the Tartars, unifying eastern Mongolia. Tuowolile, another Khan, felt threatened by the aggressive, fledgling Temujin. Relations between the two worsened. At this time, Temujin proposed a

Saddle, excavated from Genghis Khan's tomb.

marriage between his eldest son Shuchixiang and the Khan's granddaughter, but was turned down. The relations between the two grew more tense.

In the spring of 1202, the Khan falsely agreed to the marriage proposal, to woo Temujin to a banquet, and take the chance to kill him. Unexpectedly, the conspiracy was unveiled, and when the Khan launched a surprised attack, Temujin fled hastily with 19 followers. They ran to the Banzhuni River (a stretch of marshy land), where, without other inhabitants or food, they had to drink muddy water, and shoot wild horses to appease their thirst and hunger. Those were days of extreme trial for Temujin, as he struggled to unify the whole of Mongolia. Therefore, once he accomplished unity, all these 19 people were honored with distinction.

In 1206 chieftains across Mongolia organized a grand gathering on the E'nun River. All those present made Temujin, valiant and adept at military strategy, the "Great Khan of Mongolia," addressing him respectfully as "Genghis Khan." "*Genghis*" means "powerful" in Mongolian.

Drinking water from the Banzhuni River.

# KHUBLAI ESTABLISHES THE YUAN

Khublai was the founder of the Yuan Dynasty, the Great Khan of all Mongolia. He was the grandson of Genghis Khan.

Before his death, Genghis Khan abdicated his throne to Wokuotai, his third son. After Wokutai died, there were a series of power struggles within the clan, and Genghis Khan's fourth son Tuolei became heir to the throne. Later Mengge, Tuolei's son, succeeded. He placed his younger brother Khublai in charge of military and administrative affairs of the entire north, so he was able to become acquainted with learned Han intellectuals, such as the monk Liu Bingzhong, the scholars Zhang Wenqian, Hao Jing and Yao Shu, who became the top advisers whom Kublai trusted most. Liu Bingzhong said to Khublai, "The ancients said, 'One can seize, but cannot administer, a state on horseback.' On horseback, Genghis Khan, powerful and invincible, swept over 40 states and established his huge empire in a matter of a few years. However, to administer a country, a monarch has to depend on systems and regulations, on traditional ethics." Hao Jing said, "Today, whoever makes proper use of educated officialdom and adopts the traditional principles of running the country, would become emperor of all China!" To Khublai, who cherished the desire to rule all of China, these remarks were enlightening. He thus made up his mind that, once he was in power, he would practice "Han Laws" and rule the entire country by adhering to the feudal ruling system deeply rooted in the Central Plains.

To lay a solid foundation, in Longgang on the north banks of the Luanhe River (now northwest of Duolun County, Inner Mongolia), Khublai had Liu Bingzhong inspect divine geomantic signs, survey the terrain and build clusters of palaces and residences. A new city, named Kaiping, thus took shape. This was Khublai's base area, where he gathered a coterie of his top advisers.

In 1258 Mengge suddenly died from an illness in the town of Diaoyu (today's Diaoyu Hill, east Hechuan, Sichuan Province). Some say that he was seriously wounded by a flying rock, and died

⌄ Alibuge's surrender.

upon returning to camp. The death of the commander-in-chief left the soldiers with low morale. This was followed by incessant torrential rains. The scaling ladders, used by the Mongolians to charge up the city walls, snapped and broke one by one. They were forced to retreat.

Khublai followed the strategy mapped out by Hao Jing, one of his top advisers. In the spring of 1260, he rushed to his base Kaiping, and summoned the princes and aristocrats who supported him. He declared his accession to the throne, and according to Han practice, called it the "1st year of the Zhongtong reign."

The news of Mengge's death reached the plains, and one of his brothers, Alibuge, quickly took steps to usurp power. He proclaimed an amnesty

A copper cannon (replica). a powerful weapon from the Yuan Dynasty. The Mongolians, in the western expedition, used cannon to fire on castles in Central Asia and Europe.

and promoted his supporters to positions at various levels, while also sending troops to occupy Yanjing and Shanxi, aligned to block Khublai's north advance. He never expected that Khublai had been even quicker, ascending to the throne in Kaiping. Abulige could do nothing but convene a conference in Helin (today's Harhelin, Mongolia), where he proclaimed himself "Great Khan."

After suppressing Alibuge's resistance, Khublai moved the political center from Helin to the Central Plains. At that time, a group of conservative Mongolian aristocrats were resolutely hostile to Khublai's adherence to "Han Laws." Some vassals even dispatched envoys to the court, to sternly question Khublai: "Mongolia is different from Han in customs and systems. Now you have shifted toward the Han and built palaces and cities. You are following their regulations and systems. What are your intentions behind this?" Khublai, defying their threats, remained steadfast in implementing "Han Laws" to remold Mongolia.

In 1271, amidst incessant military victories over the Southern Song, Khublai, on the advice of Liu Bingzhong, based on the term *"qianyuan"* (maximum) in the *Yi Jing* (*I-Ching* or *The Book of Changes*),[1] changed the name of Mongolia to "Da Yuan." (Great Yuan). The Yuan Dynasty (1271-1368) was thus formally founded, and Khublai became the first emperor. The following year, he changed the name of Yanjing to Dadu and made it the capital of the country.

---

[1] *Yi Jing:* One of the five Confucian classics.

# MARCO POLO'S VISIT TO CHINA

⌃ A facsimile of *The Travels of Marco Polo*.

In the Yuan Dynasty (1279-1368), China had a great deal of close contact with the rest of the world. Many foreigners visited China during the period. The most influential visitor was Marco Polo (1245-1324) from Italy.

Marco Polo was born to a merchant family in Venice, then the capital of Italy. His father Niccolo Polo and his uncle Maffeo Polo traveled to the Golden Horde in 1260 to do trade and came across an envoy from the Il-Khanate to the Yuan Dynasty, who invited them to join him; they traveled to China together and met Kublai Khan (1215-1294), the first emperor of the Yuan Dynasty, who later sent Rabban Sawma as an envoy and the Polo brothers as deputy envoys to the Roman Curia. They took their credentials and went to request the Roman Pope to dispatch to China 100 missionaries versed in linguistics, grammar, logic, mathematics, astronomy, geography and music.

Shortly after the diplomatic mission had set off, Rabban Sawma became seriously ill and was unable to travel. The Polo brothers continued on their journey, but then received news that the Pope had passed away. They went back to Venice and planned to go to the Roman Curia after the new Pope was elected. By the time they returned home Niccolo's wife had died long before, and had left

⌄ Marco Polo paying respects to Kublai Khan, first emperor of the Yuan Dynasty.

their son Marco Polo on his own.

The Polo brothers waited for two years, but the election had still not yielded any results. To live up to the hopes of Kublai Khan, they set out again for China, this time taking Marco Polo along with them. The elder Polo brothers obtained credentials from the Roman Curia and, before starting off, fetched Holy Chrism from the Holy Land of Jerusalem (today's Jerusalem). When they arrived in Armenia, a

↑ Portrait of Marco Polo.

new Roman Pope had been elected. So they returned to Rome to meet the new Pope. However, the Pope dispatched only two missionaries to go with them to China. On their way there, the two missionaries became so frightened by the news that Armenia was at war that they handed the documents and gifts to the Polo brothers and returned to Rome. The Polo brothers finally reached Shangdu (northwest of today's Duolun County, Inner Mongolia), or Xanadu, the summer capital of the Yuan Dynasty, in 1275, three and half years after they had left Rome. At that time, Kublai Khan was spending his holidays in Xanadu. The Polo brothers presented him the letter and gifts from the Pope, as well as the Holy Chrism, and reported on their negotiations with the Pope and their experiences along the journey. Kublai Khan was so delighted he bestowed the title of honorary chamberlain on the three Polos.

Marco Polo was clever and quickly mastered Mongolian and other Eastern languages. Due to his abilities, he won the profound trust of Kublai Khan. Besides taking up a post in Dadu, capital of the Yuan Dynasty,

Marco Polo often inspected local provinces or went abroad on diplomatic missions by order of Kublai Khan. He traveled to areas in today's Shanxi, Shaanxi and Sichuan provinces, including regions inhabited by other ethnic minorities in Sichuan, Tibet, Yunnan and northern Myanmar. According to his own accounts, he once held an official post in Yangzhou. Later, Marco Polo served as an envoy to Nanyang (old name for Southeast Asia) and visited Annam (in today's Vietnam), Java and Sumatra (in today's Indonesia). He traveled in India and Sihala (today's Sri Lanka) as well.

After living in China for a full 17 years, the three Polos deeply longed for home, and returned at the end of 1295 when Venice was at war with Genoa. Marco Polo joined the Venetian fleet and was captured by Genoa in 1298. During one year of captivity, he dictated an account of his travels in Asia to a fellow prisoner and writer named Rustichello, who wrote it down and later published the world-famous book *The Travels of Marco Polo*. The book generated a great deal of attention and influence in Europe. As a result, many adventurers including Christopher Columbus (1451-1506) began to explore eastward and eventually came upon the "New World" (the Americas). The book set up a bridge for interaction between Eastern and Western cultures.

↑ Marco Polo's hometown Venice.

# MASTER WEAVER HUANG DAOPO

A folk song has been passed down in Wunijing Town, Songjiang County in the regions south of the lower Yangtze River, which goes: "Granny Huang, Granny Huang! Teach me spinning, teach me weaving, yielding two bolts of cloth from two bobbins at the same time." "Granny Huang" refers to Huang Daopo, a master weaver in the early Yuan Dynasty (1279-1368).

Although historical records on the life of Huang Daopo can hardly be found, many of the tales about her have been handed down to this day in Songjiang. It is said that she was born to such a destitute family that her parents arranged an engagement for her and sent her to live with the family of her future husband when she was still a child. In feudal China, child brides were used as maids and often had to suffer beatings and scolding. Huang Daopo could not stand the inhuman treatment and was determined to escape.

⌃ Statue of Huang Daopo.

She dug a hole in the thatched roof and climbed out of the house. She ran desperately through the vast fields despite her hunger. Suddenly, Huang Daopo saw a ship berthed at the Huangpu River in the far distance. She boarded the ship and hid in the cabin. The ship set off the next day for Yazhou (today's Haikou, Hainan Province). Huang Daopo then sought the help of the ship owner and reached Yazhou on the ship.

Hainan is home to the Li ethnic group. Li people began to grow cotton from a long time ago and are famed for their excellent weaving techniques. After arriving in Yazhou, Huang Daopo began to learn weaving skills from the Li. She gained complete mastery of the superb Li weaving techniques during her 30 years or so of living there. After becoming more and more homesick, at the age of about 50, Huang Daopo finally returned to Wunijing Town on a merchant ship. Her hometown was still the same as when she left — with food shortages, low yields

⊙ **Kesi Weaving Technique of the Yuan Dynasty**

Kesi weaving technique had been quite good in the Southern Song Dynasty, and kept developing in the Yuan Dynasty by combining with the gold threads weaving technique of the Western Territory. As the Lamaism was popular in the Yuan, so Buddhist content was added to the subjects of kesi fabrics. The kesi fabric *Third Generation of Buddha* in Paris might be weaved in this period. The Palace Museum's collections *Eight Immortals Celebrate Birthday* and *Dongfang Shuo Steals Peaches* are the representatives of the kesi fabric works of the Yuan Dynasty.

of cotton and backward weaving techniques. Huang Daopo was determined to impart her mastery to her fellow townsfolk.

The pedal loom invented by Huang Daopo, weaving three different yarns at the same time, was faster and more efficient than the handloom with only one spindle used in the past. She could produce beautiful cloth of all patterns using her jacquard loom.

After Huang Daopo's death, her townsfolk buried her in today's Dongwan Village, north of Huajing Town, and built an ancestral hall and statue to honor her. They would hold commemorative ceremonies for her at every festival. The new weaving techniques left by Huang Daopo spread to the middle and lower reaches of the Songjiang River and Yangtze River, and eventually all over China. By the Ming Dynasty (1368-1644), Songjiang had become the center of China's cotton textile industry and was said to have produced enough cloth to clothe the whole nation. Huang Daopo made an outstanding contribution to the development of China's textile industry in its early days.

Silk reeling. This was drawn according to the "Picture of Weaving and Plowing," in the *Book of Farming* by Wang Zhen.

Huang Daopo imparting weaving techniques.

# GREAT PLAYWRIGHT GUAN HANQING

Guan Hanqing, also known as Yizhaisou (Old Man Studying the Past), was honored as the best among the four well-known writers of Yuan Opera, and the greatest playwright of the Yuan Dynasty (1279-1368). He was born in Dadu (today's Beijing), capital of the Yuan Dynasty, around 1220 and died in 1300. During that period, Mongolia was in the process of destroying the Jin (1115-1234) and Southern Song (1127-1279) dynasties, with many social upheavals taking place. Born to a doctor's family, Guan Hanqing read widely and learned to write poetry and music from the time he was a child.

He was very fond of *zaju*, a poetic form of drama set to music, and with his good friend Yang Xianzhi, founded a *zaju* composing society.

Guan Hanqing wrote over 60 *zaju* plays throughout his life, almost twice as many as Shakespeare's plays. Among Guan Hanqing's works, 13 plays, including *Injustice to Dou E* (or *Snow in Midsummer*), *Rescued by a Coquette*, and *The Pavilion of Moon Worship*, 14 sets of *sanqu* (opera with tonal patterns modeled on tunes drawn from folk music) and 52 short lyrics have survived to this day. Most of those works exposed and condemned the

A facsimile of *Injustice to Dou E.*

cruelty of local tyrants and corrupt officials, and exalted the unyielding spirit of resistance of the oppressed classes. A self-portrait, "An Uncrushable Copper Pea," in one of his sets of *sanqu*, faithfully mirrors Guan Hanqing's assertive character.

Guan Hanqing's love stories are represented by *Rescued by a Coquette, Riverside Pavilion, The Pavilion of Moon Worship,* and *An Astute Girl Scorns a Love Affair.* These plays combined love stories with real life and social contradictions, rather than just setting love stories in an isolated environment, as well as devoting much space to direct and detailed depictions of enduring affection and the tortuous path of love. They embraced a broad range of social phenomena and exposed various social problems. Guan Hanqing's dramas on love and marriage all centered on the female protagonists and paid tribute to their spirit of pursuing happiness and resisting evil. For instance, *Riverside Pavilion* tells a story about a resourceful, bold female protagonist named Tan Ji'er who calmly fooled an imperial bodyguard surnamed Yang, who attempted to kill her husband and force her to be his concubine, and how she finally had him thrown into prison.

In his late years, some treacherous courtiers usurped power and committed all sorts of wickedness. Against this background Guan Hanqing created the earthshaking play *Injustice to Dou E.* This *zaju* drama presents a story about Dou E, who was sold as a child by her parents into her future husband's family, and was later wrongly sentenced to death due to a conspiracy hatched by the scoundrels Zhang Lü'er and his father with corrupt local officials. Prior to her execution, Dou E pronounced three vows. The first was of blood all spraying onto a long white silk streamer without a single drop staining the ground. The second was for a heavy snow in midsummer to cover her dead body, and the third for a severe drought lasting three years in the local district. Each of her vows came to be realized. Dou E had exclaimed, "While the Yamen has always appeared to be impartial, yet injustice is done in every case," expressing her sharp protest against feudal rule.

Guan Hanqing's *zaju* dramas demonstrate a perfect combination of ideas and art and have enjoyed popularity among readers at home and abroad. *Injustice to Dou E* has been published in many languages. In 1958 activities commemorating the 700th anniversary of the publication of Guan Hanqing's works were held worldwide.

Tan Ji'er, the female protagonist in *The Riverside Pavilion* by Guan Hanqing, disguised herself as a fisherwoman and obtained the imperial sword, token and writ from Magistrate Yang, so that Yang would not be able to persecute her husband.

Illustrations from *Romance of the Western Chamber,* the masterpiece of Wang Shifu, a famous playwright of the Yuan Dynasty.

# GUO SHOUJING AND HIS SHOUSHI CALENDAR

Guo Shoujing (1231-1316) was born to a scholar's family in Xingtai, Hebei. Influenced by his grandfather Guo Rong, an expert in mathematics and water conservancy, Guo Shoujing learned a great deal of scientific knowledge from the time he was a child. At the age of 15 or 16, he invented a bronze lotus clepsydra, which was a very accurate clock. Later, he presented the lotus clepsydra to

Kublai Khan (1215-1294), the first emperor of the Yuan Dynasty, and put forward six proposals for water conservancy. Kublai Khan thought highly of Guo Shoujing and assigned him a post in water resources management. In 1264 Guo Shoujing became known for repairing two famous ancient canals, the

⌄ Guo Shoujing hard at work.

Sundial made by Guo Shoujing. This was an instrument that was used to indicate time and the azimuth by the direction and length of the shadow cast by a central projecting pointer on a surrounding calibrated dial.

Earth to revolve around the sun. The Shoushi calendar was the first in the world's calendrical history to achieve such accuracy, 300 years earlier than the finalization of the Gregorian calendar, which became commonly used in the world.

In 1970 the International Astronomical Union (IAU) named a circular mountain on the moon after Guo Shoujing. The Chinese Academy of Sciences' Purple Mountain Observatory, in Nanjing, after it discovered four planets, named one of them after Guo Shoujing.

Tanglai and then the Hanyan.

The Daming calendar was used in China before the Yuan Dynasty united the nation in 1279. By that time the Daming calendar had been in use for more than 700 years and had become less and less consistent with the astronomical events of the day. After reunifying China, Kublai Khan decided to set up a specialized agency to revise the calendar, and appointed Guo Shoujing as its head. To make the new calendar more accurate, Guo modified and designed several astronomical instruments. Based on his actual observations and different functions of measurement, he rebuilt the complicated armillary sphere into two simplified instruments, called "abridged armilla," more precise, convenient and accurate than their predecessor.

Guo Shoujing eventually worked out a new calendar in 1281, after years of hard endeavor. Kublai Khan was extremely satisfied with the new calendar and took its name "Shoushi" from the *Collection of Ancient Texts*. The name signified that it tells people the time and helps them farm during the right seasons. The Shoushi calendar was extraordinary in terms of scientific accuracy. Guo Shoujing calculated through his calendar that a year consisted of 365.2425 days, only 26 seconds off from the exact time it takes the

Yangyi, created by Guo Shoujing, could be used to calculate the time of a solar eclipse, estimate its azimuth and magnitude, and to observe and survey the moon and its eclipse.

Model of abridged armilla. The abridged armilla, designed and made by Guo Shoujing in 1279, was a very advanced astronomical instrument in the world at that time.

# ZHU YUANZHANG FOUNDING THE MING DYNASTY

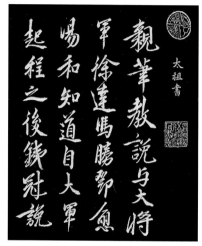
△ Detail from the *Instructions to Generals*, inscribed by Zhu Yuanzhang.

The late Yuan Dynasty (1271-1368) suffered from decadent rule, a crumbling economy, the flooding of the Yellow River and successive years of disasters. Peasants could not survive in such conditions, so large-scale insurgency broke out. In 1351 Han Shantong and Liu Futong revolted in Yingzhou (today's Fuyang, Anhui Province), and peasants in other places of the country rose up in response one after another.

In the second lunar month of 1352, landlord Guo Zixing and peasant Sun Deya rebelled in Haozhou (today's Fengyang, Anhui Province). Zhu Yuanzhang, who had been born to a destitute family and was earlier a roving monk, joined their army in the second third lunar month (there were two third month) of that leap year. Guo Zixing appreciated Zhu's valiancy and resourcefulness and married his daughter to him. When Guo died, Zhu Yuanzhang succeeded him as head of the insurrectionary army.

Seeing the discipline of Zhu's army, Li Shanchang came to seek his patronage. Zhu consulted Li about a plan for stabilizing the nation. Li told him, "Liu Bang, founder of the Han Dynasty (206 BC-AD 220), was merely a commoner when he rose up in the late Qin Dynasty (221-206 BC). As a leader who was open-minded and magnanimous, and good at judging and making use of good people while justly punishing bad people, Liu Bang ascended the imperial throne within five years. If you could follow his way, you would soon bring peace and stability to the nation." Zhu Yuanzhang applauded his advice and kept Li at his side as an advisor.

In the third lunar month of 1356, Zhu Yuanzhang seized Jiqinglu (today's Nanjing, Jiangsu Province) with his land and naval forces and renamed it Yingtianfu. In Yingtianfu he adopted the policy proposed by Zhu Sheng: "Build high walls, stock up rations, and do not be too hurried in calling yourself king." The strategy was to first fortify the rear, store abundant provisions, and not make haste in proclaiming himself king, lest he became vulnerable to attack. Zhu Yuanzhang also employed a good number of able and virtuous gener-

≫ Model of "Crow Flying with Magic Fire." This was a rocket, 45.5 cm long.

Zhu Yuanzhang devising strategies inside a command tent.

was under the control of Zhu Yuanzhang. Zhu headed for Hongdu with 200,000 soldiers. The fleets of the two sides met at Boyang Lake and began a battle lasting 36 days. In the end, Chen Youliang was killed and his army disintegrated. Zhu Yuanzhang advanced on this crest of victory and seized Wuchang.

After the elimination of Chen Youliang, no warlords in southern China dared to challenge Zhu Yuanzhang. In the first lunar month of 1364, he declared himself "King of Wu." Zhu Yuanzhang had grown from a mere nobody to an overlord within only a few years. Then Zhu annihilated Zhang Shicheng, and Fang Guozhen surrendered without a fight soon after, paving the way for Zhu's ascendancy to the imperial throne. In the years that followed, Zhu Yuanzhang, relying on his abundant financial resources in southern China and well-trained and well-disciplined army, fought battles across the country and won successive victories.

als and advisors from all over the nation, such as Liu Ji and Song Lian, assigning them to key positions.

With Yingtianfu as the headquarters, Zhu Yuanzhang captured the surrounding strongholds of the Yuan army one after another. At that time, the regions occupied by Zhu Yuanzhang bordered those by Zhang Shicheng in the northeast, Chen Youliang in the west, Fang Guozhen in the southeast and Chen Youding in the south, each of whom had proclaimed himself king and exercised control over his own region.

In the autumn of 1363, Chen Youliang led an army, claiming to number 600,000 soldiers, to attack Hongdu (today's Nanchang, Jiangxi Province), which

In early 1368 Zhu Yuanzhang proclaimed himself emperor and founded the Ming Dynasty (1368-1644). The capital was established in Yingtianfu, and Hongwu was adopted as the title of his reign. He is known in history as Ming Taizu. In the autumn of the same year, generals Xu Da and Chang Yuchuan led the Ming army to storm Dadu, capital of the Yuan Dynasty. As Yuan Emperor Shun fled northward, Yuan rule over the nation ended. It took the Ming Dynasty almost another twenty years to reunify China.

Five Thousand Years of Chinese Nation

# JINGNAN REBELLION

As his first son, Crown Prince Zhu Biao, had died before him, Zhu Yuanzhuang in his will passed the throne on to his grandson Zhu Yunwen, who became known as Ming Emperor Jianwen (r. 1399-1403). Soon after Zhu Yunwen became emperor, he saw the great power of the princedoms as a severe threat to central government, and thus adopted a proposal for reducing the number of princedoms. His action met with protest from the princes, among whom the Prince of Yan expressed the fiercest opposition.

The Prince of Yan, named Zhu Di, was the fourth son of Zhu Yuanzhang. He was conferred the title Prince of Yan in 1370, with Beiping (today's Beijing) as his domain. Zhu Di, a strapping fellow, was conversant in military strategy as well as possessing rich practical experience in commanding troops in battle. Moreover, he was cordial to his subordinates. Thus Zhu Di had high reputation in the army. Zhu Yuanzhang, who took pride in such an excellent son, often sent him to lead troops to fight battles, and handed him military power in the border areas. Thereafter the Prince of Yan enjoyed great prestige.

When Emperor Jianwen was about to have Zhu Di arrested, it occurred to Zhu Di that certain outstanding loyal officials, mistakenly accused by his father, had pretended insanity and thus avoided execution. So Zhu Di feigned madness and ran around behaving like a lunatic in Beiping. He would grab the wine and food of others when hungry; sometimes just lay on the ground and dozed off all day long. However, the imperial court only pressed him harder and harder, so that Zhu Di could no longer continue

172

to play the fool, but had to rise up and fight back.

When Zhu Yuanzhang was conferring the title of prince on his sons, he said, "All the princes should dispatch troops to kill any treacherous officials in the imperial court." His words were of great avail to the Prince of Yan, who proclaimed that there were treacherous officials in the imperial court, and that they should be eradicated to relieve the jeopardy the court found itself in. The next day, he rallied troops in Beiping under the slogan "Jingnan (Restoring Peace and Stability)," to pledge their resolve before the war. After this, Zhu Di and his nephew Emperor Jianwen resorted to arms and fought a four-year civil war, known in history as the Jingnan Rebellion.

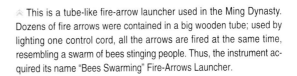

⚞ This is a tube-like fire-arrow launcher used in the Ming Dynasty. Dozens of fire arrows were contained in a big wooden tube; used by lighting one control cord, all the arrows are fired at the same time, resembling a swarm of bees stinging people. Thus, the instrument acquired its name "Bees Swarming" Fire-Arrows Launcher.

Zhu Di, boasting abundant battle experience, was valiant and well versed in military tactics. He seized large areas around Beiping in less than twenty days, and troops with tens of thousands of soldiers defected to pledge allegiance to him. Emperor Jianwen replaced his commander-in-chief Di Bingwen with Li Jinlong, and assembled an army of 500,000 soldiers to attack the Prince of Yan.

Thereafter the two sides fought many battles.

⚞ Jingnan Rebellion.

The troops of the Prince of Yan won successive victories, and kept pushing southward. They bypassed Nanjing, then capital of the Ming Dynasty, and defeated the imperial army at Linbi (today's Lingbi, Anhui Province). Next, Zhu Di's troops took Sizhou (southeast of today's Sihong, Jiangsu Province) and made offerings to their ancestral tombs. They crossed the Huaihe River and captured Xuyi (today's Xuyu, Jiangsu Province), and then moved on to Yangzhou. At that time, the imperial court was in total disarray. Some ministers and high officials, unwilling to be involved in the internal feuds, fled on various excuses, one after another.

In 1402 Yan troops arrived at Pukou (in today's Nanjing, Jiangsu Province). Zhu Di led his troops across the river and broke through the defenses of Sheng Yong. Finally, he reached the city gates of Nanjing. Zhu Hui, the Prince of Gu and Li Jinglong opened Jincuan Gate and surrendered. The Yan troops then stormed into the city.

Persuaded by civil and military officials, Zhu Di stepped onto the throne, and after his death was given the title Taizong (1360-1424). He also acquired the posthumous name Chengzu during Ming Emperor Jiajing's reign (1522-1566). Thus he was later referred to as Ming Chengzu. By 1402 the four-year civil war finally ended.

# THREE MING LITERARY CLASSICS

The social and economic development of the Ming Dynasty fostered a boom in novel writing. *The Three Kingdoms*, *Outlaws of the Marsh*, and *Journey to the West*, three of the four best-known classics of Chinese literature, were created during this period.

Luo Guanzhong, author of *The Three Kingdoms*, was a native of Taiyuan, Shanxi (although others claim of Qiantang, Zhejiang). *The Three Kingdoms* depicts the corrupt politics of the late Eastern Han Dynasty (AD 25-220), when people rose up in succession to set up separate regimes. The Three Kingdoms, Wei, Shu and Wu, ruled by Cao Cao, Liu Bei and Sun Quan respectively, gradually emerged as the three largest powers, leading to a three-way confrontation. In the end, Wei was succeeded by the Western Jin Dynasty (265-317), which later eliminated the Shu and Wu. China was reunified and came under the control of the Sima family. *The Three Kingdoms* recounts tortuous yet fascinating historical stories in succinct language, featuring vivid dialogue. It had a tremendous influence on the historical novels of later ages.

⩖ Guan Yu beheaded Huang Xiong before a cup of hot wine had cooled. This is a famous anecdote from *The Three Kingdoms*. Warlords around the country formed a coalition against the tyrannical warlord Dong Zhuo. After slaying several generals of the coalition, Hua Xiong, a military commandant under Dong Zhuo, seemed invincible. Guan Yu, who was a mere mounted archer, then volunteered to fight a duel with Hua Xiong. Cao Cao, one of the eighteen coalition leaders, poured Guan Yu a cup of hot wine but the latter declined, claiming he would soon return. Within moments Guan Yu returned with Hua Xiong's head in hand, while the wine was still warm.

△ Zhongyi Hall, a setting from *Outlaws of the Marsh*. Rebels of Liangshan Marsh won successive victories over the government army after Song Jiang was elected their leader. Heroes from other places one after another submitted to his leadership. So the Liangshan stronghold became increasingly powerful. To justify the Liangshan assembly and uprising, Song Jiang changed the name of Juyi (Assembly of Heros) Hall to Zhongyi (Loyalty and Justice) Hall.

*Outlaws of the Marsh*, by Shi Naian, has enjoyed equal fame to *The Three Kingdoms*. It presents a full view of the rise and fall of the peasant revolts led by Song Jiang in the late Northern Song Dynasty (960-1127). The novel molded a large number of archetypal characters, such as the upright, outspoken and intrepid Li Kui and righteous, unconstrained and unyielding Lu Zhishen, each displaying a distinctive and impressive personality. *Outlaws of the Marsh* was very popular among the common people due to its vivid, easy-to-understand language.

*Journey to the West*, a combination of popular and scholarly literature, appeared after the earlier two novels in the mid- to late Ming Dynasty. *Journey to the West* is a great work of imagination, telling stories of combat between deities and evil spirits. It focuses around the story of Sun Wukong, the Monkey King, who escorted the Tang monk Xuanzang to fetch the Buddhist scriptures in India, overcoming 81 challenges along the way. *Journey to the West* became a much-loved romantic novel for its grand structure and miraculous tales full of rich imagination.

△ Qing-dynasty illustrations for *Journey to the West*.

# ZHENG HE'S MARITIME VOYAGES TO THE WESTERN SEAS

Zheng He (1371-1433) was a voyager and diplomat of the Ming Dynasty. His family name was Ma, given name He, and childhood name San Bao. In 1382 Ming troops attacked Yunnan, and seized the ten-year-old Zheng He. He was taken back to the Ming camp, and castrated, to become a eunuch. He was then bestowed to Zhu Di, the Prince of Yan. Bright and diligent at studies, Zheng He became adept at military strategies and tactics. After achieving many military feats in the Battle of Jinnan, he was eventually promoted to Grand Imperial Eunuch.

In 1405, after full preparations, Zheng He set out to begin special maritime missions for Emperor Cheng Zhu. The chosen auspicious day was 15th, 6th lunar month, at Port Liujia (today's Liuhekou in Taicang County, Jiangsu Province), where vast multitudes came to send him off. To the deafening sound of gongs and drums, Zheng He, waving goodbye to officials and common people, boarded the largest ship, which followed the fleet sailing

Zheng He meeting an African chieftain.

Zheng He.

slowly eastward.

Departing Port Liujia, Zheng He's fleet sailed past Fujian, Zhancheng, Java island (now part of Indonesia), to the Port of Jiu (now Palembang, Sumatra, Indonesia), where they suddenly encountered a raid by pirates. Zheng He, commanding his fleet, defeated the pirates and captured alive their ringleader Chen Zuyi.

Southeast of the Indian Peninsula was a large island called "Ceylon Mountain" (today's Sri Lanka), a point through which the east-west sea routes of the Indian Ocean passed. In April 1409, Zheng He on his way back during a second sea voyage to the "Western Seas," on behalf of the Ming government, presented a temple in Ceylon Mountain with many valuables including gold and silver sacrificial vessels, Buddhist banners of woven gold, balms, candles and sandalwood. He also set up a stone tablet, known as the "Zheng He-Ceylon Tablet," which in 1910 was excavated at Galle.

In 1415, on his way back during his fourth voyage, he anchored off the Sumatran Kingdom (today's Aceh, in northwest Sumatra, Indonesia) to present a large quantity of treasures to its king. However, that night a gang tried to rob the fleet. With the help of Sumatran troops, Zheng He and his men fought bravely, and

scored a great victory over these pirates.

Between 1405 and 1433, Zheng He led his fleet to journey seven times to the "Western Seas." The twenty-eight years of voyage had exhausted his strength. In early April 1433, on his way back during his last voyage, the great voyager Zheng He died in Calicut, in the southwest Indian Peninsula (today's Kozhikode, India).

During Zheng He's seven voyages to the "Western Seas" over those years, he visited more than 30 countries in Asia and Africa. The farthest place he reached was "Malindi" (in today's Kenya), south of the equator along the east African coast, and "Manbasa" (today's Mombassa, Kenya). His voyages strengthened friendly relations between China and these countries, and promoted economic and cultural exchange. Zheng He earned himself a monumental role in the world history of navigation, with world maritime records regarding him as a great guide, since his voyages were 87 years earlier than Christopher Columbus, who first sailed to the America, 93 years earlier than Vasco Da Gama who first found the sea route to India around the Cape of Good Hope, and 116 years earlier than Ferdinand Magellan, who reached the Philippines during his first circumnavigation of the globe.

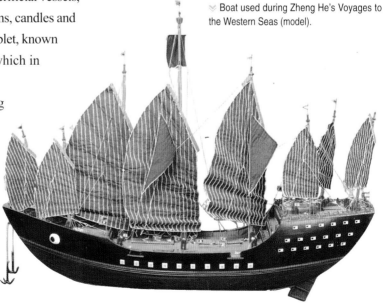

Boat used during Zheng He's Voyages to the Western Seas (model).

# THE TUMUBAO INCIDENT

The Ming Dynasty flourished during the reign of Emperors Yong Le and Xuan Zong (1403-1436), after which it began to decline. After the death of Xuan Zong (1426-1436), his son Zhu Qizhen ascended the throne. Known in history as Emperor Ying Zong, he had neither learning nor ability, placing his confidence in his favorite eunuch Wang Zhen, entrusting everything to him. Wang Zhen was tyrannical in his methods and grew to become extraordinarily powerful in the court by eliminating those who disagreed with him. Complaints among the common people were heard everywhere. Domestic troubles and foreign invasions resulted, one after another.

In July 1449, Esen, head of the Wala, a Mongolian tribe, mobilized his troops and invaded the Ming Dynasty. His troops were invincible and the defending Ming troops suffered defeats several times, with their camps and castles occupied. Military urgency forced the Ming court to send a reinforcement of 40,000 troops, led by Commandant-escort Jinyuan. However, hoodwinked by the domineering Wang Zhen, Emperor Ying Zong led an army personally to meet the invaders. Wang Zhen had believed they would achieve instant success as long as large numbers of troops were sent. Wang Zhen had imagined the victorious moment when he would invite the emperor to pass his hometown so that he might return to his hometown with fame and fortune, showing off his power and influence and bringing honor to his ancestors.

On 17 July 1449, Emperor Ying Zong assigned

⌄ Captured Emperor Ying Zong.

his brother Zhu Qiyu the task of defending Beijing, and with a huge army of 500,000 troops departed in a vast and mighty style.

Esen learned of the news, ambushed the advance troops under Jinyuan's command at the pass between two mountains, and surrounded

△ Emperor Ying Zong.

them. Hearing news of defeat, Emperor Ying Zong grew fearful and decided to retreat.

During the retreat, Guo Deng, Regional Commander at Datong, suggested that the emperor return to the capital via Zijingguan Pass. But Wang Zhen would not listen and insisted that they should retreat the way they came. When Emperor Ying Zong withdrew to Langshan, Esen and his cavalry turned up in pursuit. Dispatching Duke Zhu Yong to lead a cavalry of 30,000 to resist the attack, Wang Zhen and Emperor Ying Zong quickly fled. The emperor and his troops traveled most swiftly and arrived at Tumubao, 20 *li* away from Huailai County. The accompanying ministers requested that the emperor and his troops take refuge behind the walls of Huailai. But, because Wang Zhen had not yet arrived, Emperor Ying Zong insisted on waiting for him. However, when Wang Zhen arrived, he refused to go any further. Officials including the Minister of War recommended dividing the army in order to protect the rear and to go on high alert. To ensure the safety of the emperor, they had hoped he would hasten day and night to reach Juyongguan Pass. But Wang Zhen refused to accept this wise advice. Instead, he ridiculed the Minister of War as a pedant who knew nothing about military deployment, and decided that the army should stay overnight at Tumubao.

Taking advantage of the terrain at Yaoerlin in Langshan, Esen launched attacks from the flanks. He annihilated most of Duke Zhu Yong's army and pursued the rest all night to Tumubao, just as Emperor Ying Zong and Wang Zhen were about to leave on the second day. Upon seeing enemy troops

everywhere, they became too scared to move. With water shortages, and nothing to rely on for defense, the Ming troops, who had lost several battles, were in low spirits and fearful of engaging again with Esen's troops. A siege of three days caused many deaths of soldiers and battle horses. Confronted with a difficult situation with no food and water within, and no reinforcements from outside, the Ming troops had no other alternative but to break the siege.

The cunning Esen waited to launch flank attacks when the Ming troops spread out in lengthened formation. The Wala soldiers, long swords in hand, were in high spirits. They fought bravely and shouted to the Ming troops, "Those who take off their armor and drop their weapons shall not be killed." Thus several hundreds of thousands of exhausted Ming troops were defeated, leaving hundreds of court officials in the army, both of high and low rank, dead in the turmoil. Wang Zhen met a violent death when the General of Escort Guard Fan Zhong knocked him down with a battle hammer.

The battle at Tumubao led to the capture of Emperor Ying Zong, the destruction of hundreds of thousands of troops, as well as the deaths of hundreds of officials. History recalls this battle as "The Tumubao Incident." Afterwards, Esen used Emperor Ying Zong as a hostage to force the hand of the Ming court, on the one hand; while leading his troops to besiege Beijing, pillaging and looting everywhere, on the other hand. Esen, after the defeat by Ming troops under the command of Yu Qian, had to flee beyond the Great Wall with his unfulfilled aspiration to re-establish the Yuan Dynasty. Moreover, after the Ming court had chosen a new successor, the hostage Emperor Ying Zong was not worth as much as before. Subsequently, Esen sent an envoy to plead for peace. The Ming Dynasty also officially sent Vice Minister of Rites Li Shi with gifts to the Esen camp to have Emperor Ying Zong returned.

# QI JIGUANG'S RESISTANCE AGAINST JAPANESE PIRATES

△ Qi Jiguang.

Persecution by Japanese pirates had long existed from the early Ming Dynasty. It did not cause great trouble during the early Ming because the dynasty was strong and attached importance to sea defenses. During the reign of Emperor Jia Jing, when the commodity economy developed along the southeastern coasts, and more and more bureaucrats as well as powerful and wealthy people became involved in the sea trade, certain merchants like Wang Zhi and Xu Hai colluded with Japanese pirates to form armed gangs, and the pirates were set loose, repeatedly raiding and pillaging the southeastern coasts. The Ming government deployed a large number of troops to repel the pirates. In the resistance against Japanese pirates, there emerged many famed generals. Among them, the most illustrious was Qi Jiguang.

Qi Jiguang's style name was Yuanjing, his sobriquet, Nantang. He was born in Dongmou (today's Laiwu County, Shandong Province) in 1528, and his father was a general.

### ⊙ Strict Family Education in the Childhood

Qi Jiguang's father, Qi Jingtong, was a very righteous gentleman. Although he did not get the son until at 56, he never spoiled him. Once when the Qi Mansion needed to build a house, Qi Jingtong ordered the craftsmen to build a door with four panels for it. But the craftsmen discussed in private that the door of a general's household should be as large as having 12 door panels. The 11-year-old Qi Jiguang heard this and told his father. Qi Jingtong criticized him severely for luxuriousness. Being well brought up, Qi Jiguang always showed solicitude to his soldiers, who were therefore willing to follow him despite dangers and sacrifices.

At age 10, Qi Jiguang lost his mother and was left with only his aging sick father. Qi Jiguang led an impoverished life, which forced him to learn many things, and he matured quickly. When he was 17, his father died of illness. He succeeded his father, serving as assistant military commissioner at Dengzhou (today's Penglai County, Shandong Province).

In 1556, the 28-year-old Qi Jiguang was appointed vice regional commander in charge of the defense of Ningbo, Shaoxing and Taizhou (around today's Linhai County, Zhejiang Province) against Japanese pirates.

Over the next two years, Qi Jiguang earned his reputation after two victories at Cengang then Taizhou, but he still felt that complete reforms should be carried out within his military troops, among whom some army ruffians had become corrupted by bad habits. Based on this situation, Qi Jiguang repeatedly reported to his superiors that he wanted to recruit a new army. Shortly afterwards, he formed a new army of over 3,000, called the Qi army.

After its founding in 1561, the Qi army defeated the Japanese pirates many times. In battles of over one month, the Qi army achieved great victories, with more than 1,400 Japanese pirates annihilated. After the victory of Taizhou, Qi Jiguang also recruited 3,000 militia from Yiwu, Zhejiang, and thus the total number of the Qi army reached 6,000.

Next autumn, Qi Jiguang led his army southwards

to Fujian. There was a small island called Hengyu, more than 20 *li* northeast of Ningde County, Fujian. Between Hengyu and the mainland were shallow beaches, which were marshes at the ebb, and became sea with high tide. The Japanese pirates were stationed there, and had built a fort as well as a wooden fortress. In order to annihilate them, Qi Jiguang, after studying the terrain, first called on the pirates to surrender at Zhangwan, an important land stronghold for those stationed at Hengyu, and then launched an attack as the tide fell. Qi Jiguang told his soldiers: "We will launch an attack at ebb tide, and must exterminate all of them before high tide; otherwise we would have no way to go. Do you have the nerve?" The soldiers shouted in response: "We do!"

After reaching the beaches of Hengyu, they found that the Japanese pirates had long prepared their fortifications. However, the Qi army forged ahead and ferociously attacked the enemy positions. The two sides resorted to hand-to-hand combat. Soon the Qi army had overwhelmed the Japanese pirates, and killed them all, reclaiming the sovereignty of Hengyu, which had been occupied by the Japanese pirates for three years.

From that point on, after consecutive years of battles, the scourge of Japanese pirates along the southeastern coasts was nearly eliminated.

» Large Fu ship (model), also called "*Bai Cao.*" It acquired the name "Fu ship" because it was manufactured in Fujian. It served as the main battle ship of the Ming naval force in the southern seas.

« Qi Jiguang's resistance against Japanese pirates.

# LI SHIZHEN AND THE *COMPENDIUM OF MATERIA MEDICA*

Li Shizhen (1518-1593) was a great medical expert of the Ming Dynasty. He was born into a family of medical practitioners over generations in Qizhou, Huguang (today's Qichun, Hubei Province), in 1518. His grandfather and his father were both eminent local physicians. Nurtured in this noble family possessing generations of medical practice, unconsciously influenced by what he constantly heard and saw, Li Shizhen began to show a deep interest in medicine from childhood.

During his spare time, between bouts of reading, with a basket on his back he followed his father and brother to nearby mountains and lakes, helping to gather various types of herbs. He had possessed the ability to identify herbs since childhood. He learned a great deal about medicine by listening and helping to write prescriptions when his father was treating patients.

He discovered errors and omissions in the medical books of his time, and felt it necessary to revise them. He categorized and summarized his predecessors' as well as his own medical knowledge including his new experiences. He developed a clear outline, unified the style of writing, and presented texts with illustrations. Alongside textual knowledge, Li Shizhen focused more on outdoor herb gathering as well as field investigations, thus solving many difficult problems. Despite the difficulty of the work, he carefully identified each type of herb, and made a detailed record.

In 1561 Li Shizhen was 44 years old. He returned from the north to his hometown in Hubei, and started compiling the *Compendium of Materia Medica*. During his compilation, he still treated poor people, and conducted several field investigations. The *Compendium of Materia Medica* was a grand medical monograph, rich in content, featuring texts with illustrations. He amended it three times, and completed it in 1578. It was a summary of his predecessors' pharmacological heritage as well as a reflection of the new achievements in medical science and pharmacology of the Ming Dynasty.

At the age of 73, Li Shizhen's work was eventually recognized by a bookseller named Hu Chenlong, who knew medicine and promised to print it. In the early autumn of 1593, Li Shizhen died at 76, before, to his great disappointment, he was able to see his work printed. He was buried on the south shore of Yuhu Lake, Qizhou.

Three years later, *Compendium of Materia Medica* was first published in Nanjing. When Emperor Shen Zong issued orders to compile the history of the Ming Dynasty, Li Jianyuan, the son of Li Shizhen, presented the book to the Ming court. After the recommendation of Zhang Juzheng, head of the Inner Chancery, Emperor Shen Zong understood its practical value and ordered it printed throughout the whole country. From then on, *Compendium of Materia Medica* became popular nationwide, quickly selling out upon each block-printing, and spread far to foreign countries. It was said that over decades, it was domestically block-printed over 30 times, and nine times in Japan. Later on, it was translated into many foreign languages, including English, French, German and Latin, and circulated throughout the world.

》 Li Shizhen conducting a field investigation, keeping detailed records.

# GREAT VICTORY AT NINGYUAN

In the late Ming dynasty, the Nüzhen tribes began to rise in the northeast of China. Nurhachi, chief of one of the tribes, unified all the other Nüzhen tribes and in 1616 established his regime of the "Later Jin." In 1618 Nurhachi pledged his resolve at Zhengming, to establish the Qing Dynasty, before setting out on his arduous mission. The rise of the Nüzhen tribes frightened the Ming government, which sent armies to suppress them. A fierce battle at Sarhu between the two sides ensued. The result was that the Ming troops suffered a great defeat, and the Later Jin became even stronger.

Nurhachi captured over 70 cities east of the

⌄ Yuan Chonghuan commanding his soldiers to fight against the Qing troops during the Great Victory of Ningyuan.

⌃ Iron cannon at Shanhaiguan Pass, during the Ming Dynasty.

Liaohe River. Shortly afterwards, he commanded his army westward, and with the help of surrendered Ming generals from inside, captured Guangning (today's Beizhen County, Liaoning Province) without having to fight a battle.

After the horrible news, chaos seethed in the Ming capital. At this critical moment, an official from Ministry of War, nearly 40 years of age, rode by himself to just outside the Shanhaiguan Pass, to study the terrain. He was Yuan Chonghuan, the patriotic general remembered by posterity.

Yuan Chonghuan's style name was Yuansu. He possessed unusual courage and resourcefulness. He put himself forward to take on the task of defending Liaodong. The Ming court immediately promoted him more than one rank at a time, and ordered him to take charge of the defense of Liaodong.

In the 1st lunar month of 1626, Nurhachi led his army across the Liaohe River and arrived near Ningyuan. He sent a messenger to persuade Yuan Chonghuan using both threat and temptation: "I have sent a vast army of 300,000. Isolated Ningyuan cannot resist attack. If you surrender, we promise you a high position as well as great remuneration." After driving away the messenger, Yuan Chonghuan concentrated the military-civilian defenses, and inspired everyone to fight unto death. He made a cut on his own finger, writing a vow in blood to rouse their battle spirit.

On 24th, the Later Jin soldiers launched their attacks. After a burst of drum beats, the military-civilian defenders stood on the city wall, throwing down gunpowder barrels, battle logs and rocks, and set fire to the enemy's war chariots. After several rounds of charging, the Later Jin army could do nothing more than repelling the attacks. On the second day, Nurhachi started an even more ferocious attack and made several holes in the city wall. Yuan Chonghuan ordered the deployment of eleven newly mounted foreign cannons, and stood on the city wall to command the firing of those cannons. The Later Jin soldiers were hit by the cannonballs, which caused great casualties. Nurhachi was also wounded and had to withdraw. This became known in history as the "Great Victory of Ningyuan."

Nurhachi retreated to Shenyang, where he had moved the capital in 1626. He sighed with emotion: "I had fought numerous battles since the age of 25, and achieved victory each time. Why could I not conquer this lone city of Ningyuan?" After this defeat, with his growing melancholy and worsening wounds, this Nüzhen hero died in 8th lunar month.

⌄ Chariot with rockets.

# EUNUCH WEI ZHONGXIAN

⌃ Wei Zhongxian.

Wei Zhongxian was born in Suning, Hejian (today's Suning County, Hebei Province). He was a scoundrel who led a life of dissipation from the time he was very young. Owing to heavy gambling debts, he lived in hiding here and there. Eventually, he found no way out but to make up his mind to castrate himself and become a eunuch. He thus managed to find work in the Imperial Palace.

After the death of Emperor Guang Zong, the son Zhu Youxiao ascended the throne and became Emperor Xi Zong, and placed his confidence in Wei Zhongxian, who colluded with the emperor's wet nurse Ke to drive away the two experienced eunuchs Wang An and Wei Chao who had once promoted him. With the assistance of Ke, the totally illiterate Wei Zhongxian replaced Wang An as Director of Ceremonies.

After Wei Zhongxian had seized great power through the court, on the one hand he tried to please the young emperor by looking for and buying toys from the outside and inducing him to become caught up in cockfighting and dog-racing; on the other hand, he placed his diehard followers in the court, and persecuted those who disagreed with him in the court.

Yang Lian, Vice Censor-in-chief of the Left, was responsible for investigation and discipline of court officials. Wei Zhongxian and his eunuch

≫ Many officials tried to flatter Wei Zhongxian, to whom memorial temples were built throughout the country. Civil and military officials bowed before his statue like they were worshipping a god.

clique, greedy and tyrannical, abused power and had honest court officials dismissed, degraded, and even wrongfully put to death. At this, Yang Lian became outraged, and presented an impeachment report listing twenty-four charges against Wei Zhongxian and his partisans. Wei Zhongxian cried in front of the young emperor, with the wet nurse Ke speaking in favor of him, and other eunuchs echoing their support. The naive emperor believed Yang Lian to be in the wrong and issued an imperial order to criticize him harshly, which outraged other honest court officials. Seventy other officials submitted written reports regarding the illegal acts of Wei Zhongxian and his clique. Wei Zhongxian became utterly discomfited, while quietly pledging to eliminate them. His follower Gu Bingqian guessed Wei's mind and secretly presented a "blacklist," accusing those officials in opposition with trumped-up crimes such as forming cliques for personal gain, dominating the court, and fashioning them as members of the "Donglin Faction."

Following the blacklist, Wei Zhongxian purged the court of "Donglin Faction" members by threatening high officials to force them to resign, and by persecuting other lower officials with various means including court-ordered flogging, expulsion into exile, banishment and dismissal from office. One hundred officials were thus purged from the court. In order to eliminate them, he goaded his clique to further deal with the dismissed officials by setting them up, imputing fabricated crimes against them and involving others in those crimes. The first arrested was Yang Lian, whom Wei Zhongxian hated the most. Then, people such as Zuo Guangdou and Wei Dazhong were arrested. Wei Zhongxian and his clique tortured them using the cruelest punishments, and many of them died miserably in prison.

After the large-scale purge to eliminate court officials, Wei Zhongxian became the one who truly dominated the court. Many students from the National University flattered Wei Zhongxian by submitting written reports to the emperor about Wei's achievements and virtues, saying that the country was well managed with his assistance, and thus demanding the establishment of statues and memorial temples in his honor. The foolish emperor agreed. Those officials who wanted promotions strove to be the first to establish memorial temples for Wei Zhongxian while he was alive. Such temples were built in Beijing, for example.

After a seven-year reign, Emperor Xi Zong died and was succeeded by his brother Zhu Youjian, known as Ming emperor Si Zong with reign title Chong Zhen. Aware of the ruin that Wei and his clique had brought on the Ming court, the new emperor executed Wei's accomplices. Wei Zhongxian committed suicide, dreading punishment for his crimes.

# HUANGTAIJI'S CLEVER USE OF THE STRATEGY OF SOWING DISCORD AMONG ENEMIES

After the battle of Ningyuan, Nurhachi died and was succeeded by his eighth son Huangtaiji, who became the Qing emperor Tai Zong (1627-1644). After ascending the throne, Huangtaiji first named his new reign "Great Qing," and made preparations for attacking the Ming. However, the Ming government had long lost its vigor because of Wei Zhongxian's abuse of power. At the beginning of Emperor Chong Zhen's reign, after first getting rid of Wei Zhongxian and his clique, he started to amass all efforts to make the country prosperous; in order to deal with the threat posed by the Great Qing, he appointed Yuan Chonghuan, who had made military achievements in the great victory of Ningyuan, to direct military affairs in the northeast.

Huangtaiji knew that Yuan Chonghuan, a general of such courage and resourcefulness, was the one he most admired but also hated. In order to march through Shanhaiguan Pass, he came up with a plan for deception.

In October 1629, Huangtaiji made a detour at Xifengkou, Inner Mongolia, and entered through the Great Wall. He then marched his army directly toward the Ming capital. Upon receiving information of this, Yuan Chonghuan commanded his army day and night to return to the capital. When Huangtaiji approached Jizhou City, knowing that Yuan's troops were already stationed there, he was surprised by Yuan's rapid maneuvers. Huangtaiji led his army to hurry west and approached Beijing via Tongzhou. Learning that the Later Jin army was marching westwards, Yuan Chonghuan immediately commanded his army head towards the capital to defend it. After marching two days and two nights, his army arrived at Zuoanmen Gate of Beijing with only 9,000 troops remaining.

Rumors were then spread in Beijing that Yuan Chonghuan had urged the Later Jin army to come through the Great Wall. Thus, Yuan's army, despite fighting the Later Jin army from early morning to late afternoon outside Guangqumen Gate of Beijing, could not win Emperor Chong Zhen's trust, and was not allowed to enter Beijing to rest. Yuan's troops were forced to station at the southeast suburbs of Beijing.

Huangtaiji then intentionally ordered his army to camp near Yuan's troops so that he could use the strategy of sowing discord among his enemies. There were two eunuchs captured alive by the Later Jin army when the fight occurred near the Beijing city wall. Huangtaiji ordered Regional Vice Commander Gao Hongzhong and Assistant Regional Commander Bao Chengxian to act according to their original plans. Gao and Bao re-

《 Huangtaiji's Clever Use of the Strategy of Sowing Discord among Enemies. Two generals in Huangtaiji's camp intentionally broadcasting false information in front of the captured eunuchs, regarding Yuan Chonghuan's collusion with his enemy, so that the eunuchs would pass it on to Emperor Chong Zhen.

turned to their camp, sitting close to where the two eunuchs were imprisoned. In low voices they feigned: "Today's withdrawal was a strategy. Under the secret agreement with Marshal Yuan (referring to Yuan Chonghuan) we will succeed this time." One of the eunuchs pretended to sleep, taking those words at heart. Later, after being intentionally released by the Later Jin troops, the eunuch ran back to the palace and reported to the emperor about Yuan's collaboration with the enemy.

Emperor Chong Zhen, suspicious by nature, believed the eunuch's reports to be real. He summoned Yuan Chonghuan inside the palace for a meeting on military payroll. Upon his arrival, Emperor Chong Zhen arrested him with a charge of treason. Learning that Yuan had been arrested, Huangtaiji knew he had succeeded in his strategy and withdrew his army back to Shenyang.

After Yuan's arrest, General Zu Dashou grew frightened, and fled with the army just outside Shanhaiguan Pass. About 1,500 of Yuan's troops had also fled. Emperor Chong Zhen had to ask the imprisoned Yuan Chonghuan to write to Zu Dashou. After receiving the letter, Zu Dashou and the whole army bewailed their situation, as if shaking heaven. Zu Dashou's eighty-year-old mother persuaded him: "It would be better for you to fight the enemy and make a contribution; thus Marshal Yuan's life might be saved." The whole army became inspired and determined to carry this through.

However, the self-willed Emperor Chong Zhen was so suspicious that he put Yuan Chonghuan to death in August of the following year. This patriotic general, devoted to safeguarding the country, died under false allegations and the great shame of treason. After his death, his body was buried by a friend at Guangdong Cemetary, inside Guangqumen. It was not until the establishment of the Ming's regime in the south that Yuan Chongyuan was eventually exonerated.

# DARING KING LI ZICHENG

In the late Ming Dynasty, land was owned by an outrageously small number of people. In the Taihu Lake area, 90 percent of the people had lost their lands, while the government continued to collect more land taxes. Then poor peasants were also struck by natural disasters. In 1628 the late Ming peasant rebellion broke out first in northern Shaanxi where people had suffered the greatest damage from disasters. In the peasant war, dozens of insurrectionary troops emerged, one of which was led by Gao Yingxiang. After Gao died, there were two main insurrectionary troops: one led by "Daring King Li Zicheng," and the other by Zhang Xianzhong.

Li Zicheng (1606-1645) was born into a poor family in Mizhi, Shaanxi Province. He used to herd sheep for landlords. When he grew up, he could not pay his debts, so he was caught and beaten up; then the county magistrate put him in chains and paraded him through the streets. After the late Ming peasant war broke out, Li Zicheng joined the rebels. Skilled in martial arts, as well as being an expert horseman and archer, he was a man of rare courage and resourcefulness, so he was called the "Daring General."

At that time, areas around Henan were enduring severe disasters and famine. Li Zicheng and his troops entered Henan and advocated "equalizing land and exempting grain taxes" and thus received people's support. In Henan, the rebels executed Prince Fuwang Zhu Changxun, confiscated his property and divided it among famine victims.

In 1643 Li Zicheng took possession of Xi'an. At the beginning of 1644, the peasant troops established organs of state power under the title "Da Shun." Li Zicheng's troops then marched to Beijing, and along the way publicized their policy of "exemption from taxes for three years, killing no one" and "equality in buying and selling." The people in each place warmly welcomed the peasant troops.

At dusk on the seventeenth day of the third lunar month, 1644, the insurrectionary troops captured Beijing's Zhangyi Gate, and then started to attack other city gates. Inside the city of Beijing were seething masses of people, while flashes of fire from cannons and torches lit up the night sky of the city. High officials in the city of Beijing fell into a great panic. Emperor Chong Zhen could only sigh hopelessly, thinking how he should not have been born an emperor. Yet in those final minutes, he still could not understand the prime cause of the destruction of the Ming Dynasty, attributing it only to treacherous court officials. Extreme despair made him ruthless; he forced the empress to commit suicide, killed his favorite concubine and princess with a knife, and then hanged himself on a tree in front of the Pavilion of Imperial Longevity on Wansui Hill (His Majesty's Hill), later renamed Jingshan Hill (Prospect Hill). The Ming Dynasty, created by Zhu Yuanzhang (1328-1398), finally ended after 276 years of rule, on the eighteenth day in the third lunar month in 1644.

The peasant rebels, like floodwaters bursting through a dyke, captured Beijing. At noon on the nineteenth day, peasant soldiers in a neat formation marched towards Zhengyang Gate. The commander-in-chief's flag, with the character "Chuang," fluttered in the breeze, while the hero riding a black horse and wearing a felt hat and light blue garments, repeatedly joined his hands together to express his gratitude to the people along the road. He was none other than the famous leader of the peasant troops — Li Zicheng.

≪ Intoxicated with victory, Li Zicheng and his officers became conceited and indulged in comforts. His officers even seized the favored concubine, Chen Yuanyuan, of Wu Sangui who was guarding the Shanhaiguan Pass. Enraged, Wu Sangui opened the Shanhaiguan Pass to allow in Qing troops. Li Zicheng was thus defeated and died at the age of 39.

# QING TROOPS ENTER SHANHAIGUAN PASS

The Later Jin, set up by Nurhachi (1559-1626), was the predecessor of the Qing Dynasty (1644-1911). In 1636 the eighth son of Nurhachi Huangtaiji (1592-1643) proclaimed himself emperor in Shengjing (today's Shenyang) and changed the dynastic title to "Qing." Huangtaiji died after an illness, before Li Zicheng and his Da Shun troops overthrew the Ming Dynasty in 1644, and Dorgon took over power in the Qing Dynasty.

Dorgon was the fourteenth son of Nurhachi, and had been appointed as his successor. But Huangtaiji seized power on the basis of his might. When Huangtaiji died, Dorgon was still in his prime. Dorgon chose six-year-old Fulin, Huangtaiji's son, as the emperor titled Shunzhi, and he became the prince regent, arrogating all authority to himself and controlling court affairs. When the Ming Dynasty was overthrown, Dorgon decided to march into the Central Plains. He and his troops headed towards Shanhaiguan Pass, gateway to the Central Plains.

Halfway, the Qing troops encountered two men in Ming dress, who said they had been sent by Wu Sangui, the Ming general guarding the Shanhaiguan Pass, to welcome the Qing troops. Dorgon was overjoyed at the unexpected good news, and immediately wrote a letter to Wu Sangui, promising to dispatch troops and to confer the title of king on him if he surrendered. Wu Sangui then surrendered to the Qing troops.

When Li Zicheng heard that Wu Sangui was

unwilling to surrender to his peasant troops, he himself led troops to the Shanhaiguan Pass on a punitive expedition against Wu Sangui. On the twenty-second day of the fourth lunar month, 1644, as agreed by Li Zicheng and Wu Sangui, the two parties held a decisive battle. At first, the peasant troops obtained the upper hand as they surrounded Wu Sangui's

» The Qing troops arrived at Shanhaiguan Pass.

troops. Suddenly, the Qing troops made a surprise ambush attack, the peasant troops had no time to defend themselves, thus defeating the rebels. It was then that Li Zicheng realized that Wu Sangui had surrendered to the Qing troops. He understood too well that the peasant troops were

weaker and thus decided to prepare a war of attrition against the Qing Dynasty. On the twenty-ninth day of the fourth lunar month, Li Zicheng ascended the throne and proclaimed himself emperor in the Hall of Military Prowess in the Forbidden City. On the following morning, he and his troops retreated to

Xi'an. Two days later, the mighty Qing troops arrived in the city of Beijing. When entering the city, Dorgon held a meeting in the Hall of Military Prowess. He took one look at the respected Ming officials and declared: "Our Qing troops are benevolent. This time we entered Shanhaiguan Pass only to fight the enemy to revenge your emperor." After these words, Dorgon told his Qing princes and officials: "I order that soldiers should not be allowed to break into civilians' houses after entering the city; those who violate my order will be punished." Several days later, Dorgon held a funeral for Emperor Chong Zhen, and proclaimed that he would not set himself against Ming bureaucrats and landlords.

Hearing this, the landlords and bureaucrats who had fled to the mountains, to hide from the peasant troops, jubilantly returned to their houses, with their heads shaved and wearing queues according to Manchu tradition, so as to welcome the Qing troops.

Dorgon occupied Beijing, fulfilling the long-time dream of Nurhachi and Huangtaiji. He decided to move the capital. In the tenth lunar month of 1644, Emperor Shunzhi came to Beijing from Shengjing (Shenyang). Dorgon issued an imperial edict in the name of the little emperor, proclaiming Beijing as the new capital. From then on, after starting out as a regional power in northeast China, the Qing Dynasty began to rule the whole of China.

# SHI KEFA DEFENDS YANGZHOU TO THE DEATH

In 1644, when Qing troops took over Beijing, landlords and bureaucrats in Nanjing supported Prince Fuwang, named Zhu Yousong, grandson of Emperor Shen Zong (r. 1573-1620), to establish the Hongguang reign of the Southern Ming Dynasty (1644-1645). Shi Kefa was the Minister of Rites of the Southern Ming. He was upright and incorruptible, and enjoyed great prestige. After the Southern Ming was set up, another official, Ma Shiying who harbored hatred for Shi Kefa, induced Prince Fuwang to send Shi Kefa to Yangzhou. At that time Dorgon, who wanted to make use of Shi Kefa's prestige to conquer areas south of the Yangtze River, had written many letters to Shi to persuade him to surrender to the Qing Dynasty. Shi Kefa had flatly refused.

In the fourth lunar month of 1645, Qing troops arrived 30 kilometers outside the city of Yangzhou. Hearing this, Shi Kefa, burning with anxiety and with no time to summon his guards, that very night flew on a horse to Yangzhou, accompanied by several servants. Immediately after arriving in Yangzhou, he sent people to dispatch forces.

⌃ A Qing cannon. The Qing troops gradually became equipped with cannons before they entered the Shanhaiguan Pass. The troops relied on cannons during the battles.

However, generals in nearby towns all took a wait-and-see attitude with their forces, and refused to follow Shi Kefa's orders. Only one commanding officer, Liu Zhaoji, led two thousand people to the rescue. Since his military strength was too weak, Shi Kefa ordered Liu Zhaoji and his troops to enter the city, and then closed the city gate to prepare the defenses of Yangzhou.

Shi Kefa and Liu Zhaoji themselves directed the battle at the city walls. Civilians also organized volunteers, and young and able-bodied men stood sentry at the city walls, while the elderly and women cooked for them. Soldiers and civilians in the city of Yangzhou were determined to wage a bloody battle against the enemy.

Qing troops strengthened their offensive. Although soldiers and civilians carried on a resolute defense against the enemy, they found themselves utterly isolated, with a great disparity in strength between them and the enemy. Shi Kefa understood that the situation had no chance of improving but decided to defend Yangzhou to the death. Generals and soldiers ultimately died as heroes, while Shi

Kefa was captured by the Qing soldiers.

The Qing soldiers dared not slight Shi Kefa and immediately took him to Duo Duo. Duo Duo stepped forward, saluted Shi Kefa, and said politely, "I invited Master Shi several times, yet you refused. Today your loyalty to the Ming Dynasty has ended, so please help our Qing Dynasty conquer areas south of the Yangtze River, and we will reward you kindly." Shi Kefa responded sternly, "I am a high official of the Ming Dynasty. How could I live in shame as an eternal villain? You may kill me, but I shall not bend my head!" Duo Duo pulled a long face and said, "You are a loyal official, then I shall satisfy your wish." Shi Kefa smiled and declared,

△ Shi Kefa defended Yangzhou to the death. No coercion or cajolery could shake Shi Kefa's determination, as he calmly faced death.

"I am happy even being torn to shreds. But I have one request. Please do not kill any of Yangzhou's civilians." After saying this, Shi Kefa walked down the city wall, holding his head high, to face death calmly.

Duo Duo did not fulfill Shi Kefa's request, but slaughtered Yangzhou civilians. In ten days, 800,000 people were killed, and the once prosperous Yangzhou was almost turned into a ghost city. This became known as the infamous "Ten-Day Massacre at Yangzhou."

# ZHENG CHENGGONG RECOVERS TAIWAN

Zheng Chenggong (1624-1662) was born in Nan'an, Fujian. As a young man, he took part in the struggle against Qing rule. In the coastal areas around Fujian and Guangdong, he organized non-governmental armed forces to fight Qing troops. To expel Dutch invaders and set up an anti-Qing base, Zheng Chenggong decided to recapture Taiwan.

⌃ Zheng Chenggong was a famous general who fought against the Qing in late Ming and early Qing dynasties, as well as a national hero who recovered Taiwan.

In the third lunar month of 1661, Zheng Chenggong ordered his son Zheng Jing and some troops to stay behind to guard Xiamen, while he led 25,000 officers and men on several hundred warships, setting out from Jinmen for Taiwan. At daybreak on the first day of the fourth lunar month, the fleet arrived in Luermen. Luermen was the gateway to Taiwan; numerous submerged reefs formed a "natural barrier," making it difficult for ships to pass through. Zheng Chenggong asked He Bin (a patriot who presented a map of Dutch troop positions on the island to help Zheng Chenggong recover Taiwan) to sit on the large, well-equipped central ship and guide the fleet according to the map. The fleet advanced quietly, rounding submerged reefs by turning at times to the left and at other times to the right, and passed Luermen secretly, to advance toward Heliao Port.

When Taiwan civilians heard that Zheng Chenggong's troops were coming to recover Taiwan, they ran around passing on the word and then drove ox-carts of supplies to the troops on landing. In less than two hours, all of the several thousand soldiers had landed safely. Before daybreak the Dutch heard the news. The Dutch governor of Taiwan, Fredrich Coyet promptly ordered the artillery to open fire. However, the Chinese warships followed the central ship and avoided the Dutch forts, to arrive at a place between Fort Zeelandia (today's Anping Fort) and Fort Provintia (today's Chiqian Tower), cutting off the connection between the two fortified points.

Seeing this, Fredrich Coyet hurriedly sent forces to meet Zheng's troops at sea and on land. The Dutch commander on land was the arrogant Captain Baird. He boasted: "The Chinese by nature cannot bear the smell of gunpowder and the sound of Mauser rifles. When guns are fired, they will disintegrate." First he prayed "God bless us!" and then ordered his 240 soldiers to stand in twelve rows to fire at the Zheng troops.

⌃ Rattan shields used by Zheng Chenggong's forces.

Zheng Chenggong divided his 4,000 soldiers along two routes: one to directly take on the enemy, and the other to outflank the enemy; arrows flew down at the enemy like rain. When Dutch soldiers saw the fearless Chinese people, they disintegrated before they could fire, some throwing away their rifles and fleeing. The Zheng troops then pursued

them in the flush of victory, killing Captain Baird and his 118 soldiers, capturing many weapons. Several months later, Fredrich Coyet could do nothing but surrender, and with the remnants of his army departed from Taiwan.

The recovery of Taiwan was a great victory for the Chinese people in resisting colonialism, and Zheng Chenggong thus became a national hero shining through the ages, to be praised by later generations.

⌄ Facing the spirited offensive of Chinese troops, the Dutch General ultimately signed an instrument of surrender and handed it to Zheng with great respect.

# EMPEROR KANGXI SUPPRESSES THE REBELLION OF "THREE VASSAL PRINCES"

The "Three Vassal Princes" of the early Qing Dynasty refers to Wu Sangui in Yunnan and Guizhou, Geng Jingzhong in Fujian, and Shang Kexi in Guangdong. The three had all been Ming generals guarding regions east of the Liaohe River, who later surrendered to the Qing Dynasty and led Qing troops into the Central Plains. Emperor Shunzhi conferred the title of "Prince" on them. Later, the three Vassal Princes extended their influence and threatened the rule of the Qing.

Emperor Kangxi (r. 1654-1722), also named Xuanye, was the fourth son of Emperor Shunzhi. He ascended the throne at age four and assumed the reins of government at fourteen, eliminated Ao Bai, took over power, and made vigorous ef-

Portrait of young Emperor Kangxi in informal dress. He was one of the Chinese emperors who reigned the longest and made the greatest achievements.

forts to build up a strong and prosperous country. After Emperor Kangxi assumed the reins of government, he had to always consider the problem of the "Three Vassal Princes." So, he decided to first deal with Wu Sangui.

Hearing that Emperor Kangxi was planning to dismantle the administration of the region by the "Vassal Prince," Wu Sangui sent a memorial of request of revocation of the administration of the region by the vassal prince to Emperor Kangxi in Beijing, to discover the emperor's actual thinking, though he himself believed that, upon his request, the emperor would no longer agree to dismantle the administration of the region by the "Vassal Prince." Geng Jingzhong received wind of this and immediately sent a memorial with the

The Qing troops captured the city of Kunming. In 1681 the "Rebellion of the Three Vassal Princes" was finally suppressed.

same content to Emperor Kangxi.

Then, to Wu Sangui's surprise, Kangxi agreed to his request. He was infuriated and decided to rebel against the emperor. Wu Sangui donned Ming mourning clothes and led his troops to the tomb of Zhu Youlang (1623-1662), the last emperor of the Southern Ming regime. He knelt in front of the tomb, poured wine onto the ground and kowtowed again and again. He cried his heart out, making his solders weep too.

In the same year of 1673, Wu Sangui led his troops to the north under the banner of "Restoring the Ming against Qing." Geng Jingzhong in Fujian immediately responded. Shang Kexi was forced to kill himself under the pressure of his

son Shang Zhixin, who also launched an armed revolt in Guangdong. Han warlords in Guizhou, Guangxi, Sichuan, Hunan and Hubei took over cities and seized territories in response to Wu Sangui's call. Thus Wu Sangui reached Hunan after only a few battles. In a few months, his troops took six provinces in the south without difficulty.

In the face of the rebellion, Emperor Kangxi acted with decisiveness: He sent his Eight Banner troops to suppress Wu Sangui. As for Geng Jingzhong and Shang Zhixin, Emperor Kangxi de-

⌃ The "Awesome General," a copper cannon used by the Qing troops.

ployed both soft and hard tactics. On the one hand, he sent their brothers, living in Beijing, to Fujian and Guangdong respectively, to influence them, promising not to bear any grudges; on the other hand, his Eight Banner troops went on the attack. The two rebel troops had no way out, and soon surrendered.

In the third lunar month of 1678, Wu Sangui tore off his disguise of "Restoring Ming" and proclaimed himself emperor, with the title Da Zhou for his reigning dynasty. At the capital Hengzhou (today's Hengyang, Hunan), he hurriedly held the coronation. However, Wu Sangui was opposed by the public and even deserted by his followers; and in less than five months, consumed by worry and rage, he died of sickness.

With Wu Sangui's death, the situation came under the complete control of the Qing troops. In 1681 the "Rebellion of the Three Vassal Princes" was finally suppressed after eight years.

Emperor Kangxi reigned for 61 years, and his efforts led the Qing Dynasty into its prime. When his grandson Emperor Qianlong (r. 1736-1796) took the throne, the country grew even more prosperous and strong. Therefore, people of later generations called this period, "Times of Prosperity."

⌄ A Tang-dynasty poem in Emperor Kangxi's calligraphy.

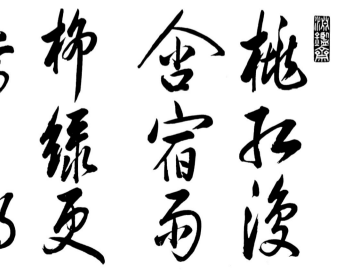

# CAO XUEQIN AND *A DREAM OF RED MANSIONS*

The book *A Dream of Red Mansions* was the most famous novel in ancient China. Mao Zedong read it many times. Its author was Cao Xueqin.

The ancestors of Cao Xueqin were of Han nationality in Liaoyang, northeast China. His family became servants of the Qing emperor at the end of the Ming Dynasty, and belonged to the Plain White Banner, one of the three Upper Three Banners (Yellow, Yellow Border and White banners). Cao Xueqin's great-grandmother was the nurse of Emperor Kangxi; after this, his family grew closer to the imperial family. After Emperor Kangxi assumed

⌄ Cao Xueqin, after falling into misfortune, wrote *A Dream of Red Mansions.*

憶縣靜日
玉生香

病稚瑛
淚灑相思地

Illustrations in an old edition of *A Dream of Red Mansions*.

the reins of government, he granted the Cao family the hereditary title of Jiangning Zhizao (Superintendent of Imperial Silk Manufacture in Nanjing) and control of the salt administration of Jiangsu and Anhui. Emperor Kangxi went to Nanjing six times on his tours of the south, staying five times at the Jiangning Zhizao Office.

However, during open strife and veiled rivalry among the sons of Emperor Kangxi, the Cao family made a misjudgment: they did not support the fourth prince Yinzhen, and instead maintained close relations with his enemy, the eighth prince. When Yinzhen ascended the throne as Emperor Yongzheng, he tried to find fault with the Cao family. Since the Cao family had long been extravagant, they embezzled public money. Emperor Yongzheng removed Cao Fu (Cao Xueqin's father) from office, charging the Cao family with embezzlement, and confiscated the Cao property. At that time, Cao Xueqin was only 13 years old, and came to Beijing with his father.

Day by day, the financial situation of the Cao family grew from bad to worse. Being used to extravagance, they had to sell off their ancestral estate not long after their return to Beijing. Cao Xueqin, too impoverished to live in the city of Beijing, was then forced to move to the countryside.

He lived in a small village at the foot of Western Hill. In his house there was only an old bed, a bench and a table. He lived on the Manchu grain rations and by selling scripts and paintings. He often only had porridge to appease his hunger.

After leaving the noisy and chaotic city, he contemplated the decline of his family and discovered that the society had grown rotten from the inside. Thus he started to write his novel *The Story of the Stone* (later renamed *A Dream of Red Mansions*), embodying his thoughts in the novel written with deliberate vagueness. Ten years later, he completed the 80-chapter book.

The novel is about four families — Jia, Shi, Xue and Wang — the despots of their area. They cruelly oppress civilians and wallow in luxury and pleasure; brothers and sisters-in-law are locked in open and smoldering strife, jockeying for position. Eventually they are reported to the authorities, and the emperor sends

people to check on and confiscate the property of the Jia family. Later, the Shi, Xue and Wang families are also brought to justice and become impoverished.

In the Jia family, an unconventional young pair, Jia Baoyu and Lin Daiyu, both dissatisfied with their situation, become bosom friends, but people around them oppose their relationship. The four families in the book are a microcosm representing the entire ruling class; while Jia Baoyu and Lin Daiyu's rebellious spirit expresses Cao Xueqin's own resentment toward the society.

Cao Xueqin devotedly poured all his experiences, conviction and talent into the novel. The novel is well constructed, the language fresh and cohesive; and the book creates many artistic char-

The wedding ceremony of Jia Baoyu. Jia Baoyu was an aristocrat, with all his needs in life met, yet he was unable to marry the girl he loved.

acters with archetypal personalities. The novel represents the zenith of Chinese classics.

After Cao Xueqin died, handwritten copies of the novel spread, and more and more people came to learn of it. This literary masterpiece became a great sensation of the time. In modern times, research on *A Dream of Red Mansions* became a specialized subject called "*Hongxue*" ("Red" Studies), while experts studying the novel are called "Hongxuejia" (Red Studies specialists). There are many such specialists in China and abroad.

# LIN ZEXU DESTROYS OPIUM AT HUMEN

After the times of prosperity in the reign periods under Emperor Kangxi and Emperor Qianlong, officials and civilians of the Qing Empire started to dream of the "Celestial Empire," and the government upheld the policy of closing the country to the rest of the world. However, at that time Western countries had already embarked on a new path to development. To put an end to the trade deficit, these countries started to smuggle opium into China in order to degrade the Chinese people.

> Lin Zexu.

Opium is a type of drug made from the milk of the poppy, and strongly toxic. A little opium can ease pain, reduce diarrhea and relieve cough; but anyone who takes it becomes easily addicted, until they need to take it every day. Statistics in 1835 showed that two million Chinese people took opium at that time, and more than four million taels of silver flowed to Western countries. Essentially, opium harmed the Chinese people, and moreover caused a great loss to the financial revenues of the Qing Dynasty.

In early 1839, Emperor Daoguang (r. 1821-1851) sent his imperial commissioner Lin Zexu (1785-1850) to Guangzhou. Lin was determined to ban the opium trade. Using all means possible, Lin Zexu acquired a good understanding of opium smuggling and severely punished certain officials, soldiers and opium traders. He then promulgated an announcement, declaring that all foreign businessmen should turn in all their opium and sign

⩔ The scene of opium destruction at Humen, engraved on the Monument to People's Heroes at Tian'anmen Square in Beijing.

⌃ Lin Zexu in charge of destroying opium at Humen.

letters of guarantee to never again engage in opium smuggling. If they were still found to be engaged in the opium trade, they would be punished accordingly: the opium would be confiscated and the criminal executed.

At the news, foreign opium smugglers living in the Guangzhou Foreign Building became alarmed and confused, and some immediately turned over their opium. Yet, incited by British Commercial Supervisor George Elliot, others plotted to refuse to turn in the opium.

Hearing this, Lin Zexu ordered decisively: "Send an announcement immediately to the British merchants — According to our practice, they have refused to turn over the opium but plan to evade the law; thus the Chinese government must stop the trade between China and Britain. We should dispatch troops to blockade the building, withdraw Chinese personnel from it, and cut off transportation to the sea. If they still resist, we shall stop the supply of food. And our navy will keep close watch on British ships."

Therefore, the British merchants turned over their opium. All the opium totaled over 20,000 boxes (including 1,500 boxes from US merchants) and weighed 2,370,000 *jin* (about 1,185,000 kg). Lin Zexu decided to destroy the opium publicly on Humen beach. This lasted more than twenty days, after which time all the opium Lin Zexu had confiscated had been completely destroyed.

⌃ A couplet written by Lin Zexu.

Five Thousand Years of Chinese Nation

# THE FIRST OPIUM WAR

The burning of opium stocks in Humen gave Great Britain an excuse to launch a war against China in 1840. As soon as Lin Zexu arrived in Guangzhou, he had started to train the soldiers and consolidate defenses, adding over 200 cannons. He also organized local fishermen and salt producers to fight back if attacked by foreign invaders. With such extensive preparations, it was not surprising to see the Anglo invaders fail in Guangzhou.

When British troop first attacked Guangzhou, the British government deployed 48 warships and 4,000 (later increased to 10,000) marines and

⌄ Chen Huacheng leading his soldiers to fight bravely.

infantry, led by the Elliot brothers. The attack was repelled by Chinese locals and soldiers before the British could even set foot onshore. With the ebb tide in their favor, Chinese local residents, fishermen and soldiers launched an offensive

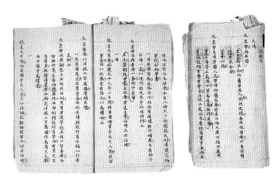

Copy of the "Treaty of Nanjing."

from small boats and burnt many of their warships, using fire arrows and other fire weapons. After that, British troops were afraid to stay too close to shore, and only hovered about at sea.

Since British troops could not touch Guangzhou, they went north to try to find a weak area to attack. They chose the Dinghai (in today's Zhoushan Islands) in Zhejiang, and Baihekou in Tianjin. Emperor Daoguang and the Qing government became terrified as the British invaders approached. The treacherous officials who opposed the ban on opium protested to the emperor, that Lin Zexu had offended the foreigners by burning opium and called on the emperor to punish him.

As a result, Emperor Daoguang issued an edict to dismiss Lin Zexu from his post, and sent Qi Shan to negotiate with the British enemy. As soon as Qi Shan arrived in Guangzhou, he removed the marine defenses, reduced the soldiers and ships, and dismissed the local fishermen newly recruited by Lin Zexu. Encouraged by these senseless actions, British troops took over the Humen emplacement without any effort. This resulted in high casualties among patriotic Chinese officials and soldiers. After that, Emperor Daoguang had to replace Qi Shan with Yi Shan.

Unfortunately, Yi Shan was no different from Qi Shan, a coward. After arriving in Guangzhou, he rushed to take

on the British troops. When the British troops fought back, he took fright and fled back to Guangzhou. The British enemy thus easily took over Guangzhou. He then sent Guangzhou governor Yu Baochun to sue for peace, and signed the "Treaty of Guangzhou," which promised to withdraw Qing government troops out of Guangzhou, and compensate British troops with 6 million yuan to redeem Guangzhou.

The Qing government's cowardice and concessions hastened British invasion. The British government sent more troops for further incursions. Subsequently, both the British and Chinese sides launched even more intense battles along the southeast coastal cities.

In the spring of 1842, British troops attacked Wusongkou at the estuary of the Yangtze River, and then took over Shanghai, Baoshan and Zhenjiang.

After Zhenjiang had been invaded, the Qing government, deathly terrified, decided to surrender. That is how the first unequal treaty in China's modern history — the "Treaty of Nanjing" — came into being.

A Qing-dynasty gunboat (model) during the Opium War.

# TAIPING REBELLION

⌃ Hong Xiuquan.

The narrow-minded, corrupt and decadent Qing Dynasty had finally aggravated the Chinese people so much, that they rose in rebellion. The year of 1851 witnessed the largest peasant rebellion in Chinese history, the Taiping Rebellion, initiated by Hong Xiuquan.

Hong Xiuquan (1814-1864), a native of Huaxian County in Guangdong Province, was very gifted and always eager to learn new things from the time he was very young. But his talent was never appreciated by the Qing government. After failing in the imperial examinations several times, he finally lost faith in the Qing government. Once, he by chance obtained a copy of *Benevolent Words to Advise the World* from a foreign priest, and became "enlightened" upon reading it. This book provided a favorable theoretical weapon for him to call upon the masses to overthrow the Qing Dynasty. Not long after, Hong Xiuquan converted Hong Rengan of the same clan and his former classmate Feng

Yunshan, and together they traveled to many places to carry out their mission. He and Feng Yunshan established a new iconoclastic sect called the "God Worshippers" at Zijingshan in Guangxi Province. This sect attracted a group of people who also became the major force of the later Taiping Rebellion, including Yang Xiuqing, Xiao Chaogui, Wei Changhui and Shi Dakai.

On January 11 of 1851, Hong Xiuquan formally declared the rebellion and established the "Taiping Heavenly Kingdom," and his people were known as the "Taiping revolutionaries."

When Hong Xiuquan declared the uprising at the village of Jintian, more than 10,000 people responded.

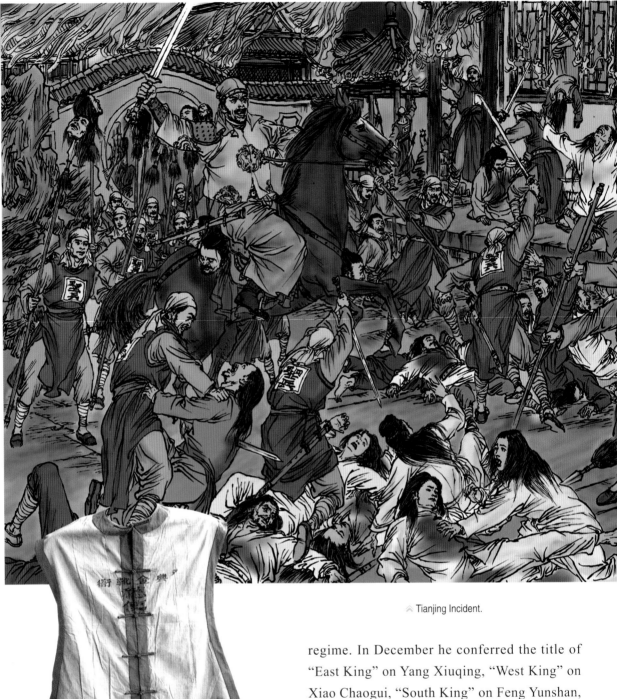

△ Tianjing Incident.

△ A type of uniform worn by the Taiping revolutionaries.

The Taiping revolutionaries defeated the imperial troops many times. On March 23, Hong Xiuquan ascended the throne at Dongxiang in Wuxuan and titled himself the "Heavenly King." He then continued to expand his power. In September he conquered Yong'an and built up his regime. In December he conferred the title of "East King" on Yang Xiuqing, "West King" on Xiao Chaogui, "South King" on Feng Yunshan, "North King" on Wei Changhui, and "Yi King" on Shi Dakai. The East King had more power than the other kings.

In a very short time, the Taiping Heavenly Kingdom conquered Wuchang, Anqing, Nanjing and other cities. They occupied Nanjing as their capital city and called it "Tianjing" (Heavenly Capital). Before they took Nanjing, the Taiping Heavenly Kingdom had never stationed troops at the places they conquered. After they estab-

lished the capital of Tianjing, they started on northern and western expansion in order to consolidate their regime, and take over the whole country.

The Taiping Heavenly Kingdom's military victories could not prevent political corruption, and the increasingly intense internal conflicts.

After the Taiping Heavenly Kingdom settled down in Nanjing, Hong Xiuquan allowed Yang Xiuqing to take charge of military power. Yang Xiuqing won many victories in battles, and became highly prestigious in the leadership. He became dissatisfied with his position, which was just next to Hong Xiuquan. Eventually, in August 1856, he forced Hong Xiuquan to abdicate. Hong Xiuquan first promised to hold a ceremony for him on Yang Xiuqing's birthday, and then secretly summoned back to Beijing Wei Changhui in Jiangxi, Shi Dakai in Hubei and Qin Rigang in Zhenjiang. On September 1, with Qin Rigang's help, Wei Changhui led a contingent of 3,000 well-trained soldiers to Yang Xiuqing's mansion. They killed Yang Xiuqing and all his family members, attendants and guards. Although Hong Xiuquan had eliminated Yang Xiuqing, he could not control Wei Changhui. He therefore supported Shi Dakai and Yang Xiuqing's former subordinates, to attack the North King's mansion and kill Wei Changhui. Hong Xiuquan's suspicious and jealous nature also led to the betrayal of Shi Dakai (in charge of state affairs). This was called the "Tianjing Incident."

In order to save this endangered regime, Hong Xiuquan started to promote a group of up-and-coming young people. Among them, two of the most important leaders were Chen Yucheng, the King of Ying, and Li Xiucheng, the King of Zhong.

In August 1860, the Qing government appointed Zeng Guofan as the imperial envoy to suppress the Taiping revolutionaries. Later, Zeng Guofan led the Xiang (abbreviation for Hunan Province) troops to launch a series of intense offensives against the Taiping Heavenly Kingdom. On 1 June 1864, Hong Xiuquan died following an illness, after Zen Guofan's troops had held him under siege. On July 19, the Xiang troops broke through the city walls of Tianjing. For three days about 100,000 Taiping revolutionaries battled to their last breath against the Xiang soldiers.

The Taiping Heavenly Kingdom lasted 14 years, conquered 18 provinces and over 600 cities, which covered more than half of China. It delivered the Qing Dynasty a heavy blow.

⌃ A horn used by Taiping revolutionaries.

⌃ Cover of the *Heavenly Kingdom's Land System*.

# THE BURNING OF YUANMINGYUAN

In 1856 the Anglo-French Allied Forces launched the second Opium War, and signed the "Treaty of Tianjin" with the Qing government.

In the spring of 1860, Britain and France concentrated more than 20,000 soldiers to attack Dagu. They occupied Tianjin, and then marched to Tongzhou, east of Beijing, which made the Qing government panic. Emperor Xianfeng (r. 1851-1862), who resided in Yuanmingyuan (old Summer Palace) in the western suburbs of Beijing, fled to Chengde with his empress, concubines, as well as a

⩔ Festive scenes of Emperor Qianlong viewing the Main Fountain are long gone; today only the ruins of the Main Fountain, destroyed by the Anglo-French Allied Forces, can still be seen. They silently sit there, serving as a voice to warn our descendents to learn from past humiliation.

group of officials. He left his brother Yi Xin, Prince Gong, to negotiate with the Anglo-French invaders.

When they arrived in Beijing, the Anglo-French Allied Forces thought Emperor Xianfeng was still staying at Yuanmingyuan, so they went around Andingmen Gate and Deshengmen Gate,

《 Ruins of Yuanmingyuan.

occupied Haidian District and then marched toward Yuanmingyuan.

Yuanmingyuan consisted of the Yuanming, Wanchun and Changchun gardens. It was first initiated during Emperor Kangxi's reign period (1662-1722) and expanded in Emperor Yongzheng's reign period (1723-1736). Emperor Qianlong enjoyed traveling. He visited Jiangnan (south of the lower Yangtze River) six times. Every time he saw some unusual rocks, he would ask people to bring them back to Yuanmingyuan. With anything he could not have moved, he would ask talented craftsmen to make a reproduction for Yuanmingyuan. The Qing emperors after Qianlong continued to expand and renovate Yuanmingyuan, making it more and more attractive.

The Anglo-French invaders broke into Yuanmingyuan, and started looting. They took away as much treasure as they could, and smashed the *nanmu* (type of high-quality wood) furniture, bronze wares and porcelain vessels that they could not carry away. The British commander T. Hope Grant supported British Lord Elgin's decision to burn down Yuanmingyuan, and said in his statement to Elgin, "In order to instill a deep impression to the Chinese government and let them know our power, it is necessary to burn down Yuanmingyuan."

Yuanmingyuan was set on fire. Its grand, luxurious and majestic palaces, pavilions, chambers and towers collapsed and perished in ashes. The exotic flowers, grasses and trees were all trampled under and destroyed. The entire imperial garden was turned into ruins. These most splendid gardens disappeared from the world forever.

After the Anglo-French Allied Forces burned

⚔ Anglo-French Allied Forces setting fire to and looting Yuanmingyuan.

down Yuanmingyuan, they built emplacements in the Ditan (Temple of Earth) area, threatening Beijing. Under pressure from Britain, France and Russia, Yi Xin accepted every condition the invaders proposed, and signed another unequal treaty — the "Treaty of Beijing." This treaty confirmed the validity of the "Treaty of Tianjin," and added further articles, such as the opening of Tianjin — the door to Beijing, and the largest port in north China — as a trading port, and to cede Kowloon to Britain. The Qing government also had to pay a huge amount of money as compensation. For the Chinese people, already suffering hardships at this time, this undoubtedly added fuel to the flames.

# DOWAGER CIXI'S POWER "BEHIND THE CURTAIN"

Emperor Xianfeng, who had fled to Chengde when the Anglo-French Allied Forces attacked, thereafter never returned to Beijing. Upon hearing the bad news from Beijing, he fell seriously ill in the Summer Resort in Chengde. In August of 1861, he made an oral testament on his deathbed to enthrone his six-year-old son Zai Chun, and to designate eight court officials, including Zai Heng, Duan Hua and Shu Shun, to assist the boy in imperial court affairs.

After Emperor Xianfeng died, the eight officials enthroned Zai Chun (r. 1862-1875) and gave the title "Qi Xiang" (Blessing and Auspice) to the little emperor's reign. Empress Niohuru was revered as the "Empress Dowager." Concubine Yi, or Yehonala, as the little emperor's mother, was honored as the "Holy Mother Empress." But Yehonala longed for control of the imperial court, and a role in power. At that time, military forces were under the eight officials' control. Yehonala knew that without military forces, she could not take power. So she and Yi Xin, Prince Gong, made an alliance with the Mongolian princes Senggelinqin and Shengbao who had military power. In this way Yehonala controlled the troops nearby Beijing. After she acquired military support, she urged the eight officials to escort Emperor Xianfeng's coffin back to Beijing. She said to the eight officials, "Zai Heng, Duanhua and the other five officials should escort us, the two empresses and the little emperor, along the shortcut back to Beijing; Shu Shun and the troops who escort the emperor's coffin should take the main road. We will arrive in Beijing first, and then we will receive you with other imperial court officials." The eight officials had no idea it was a trap, so they did what the empress said. The truth was that Yehonala was planning to separate Shu Shun, the most pow-

Cixi, whose family name was Yehonala, was the concubine of the Emperor Xianfeng. She was conferred as Yi Guifei (high-ranked imperial concubine) and lived in the Chuxiu Hall as she gave birth to a son named Zaichun for the emperor. Later, when her son Zaichun acceded to the throne as the Emperor Tongzhi, she became Empress Dowager, conferred as Holy Mother Empress Dowager. In 1861, she mounted the Xinyou Coup and then attended to court affairs from behind a curtain. She in fact controlled the country. With her great effort, the Qing Dynasty was temporarily in a stable state, praised as "Golden Years of Tongguang." However, in her late years, she was very afraid of foreign powers, and sold out the country's sovereign for their favors. She died in 1908, and the Qing Dynasty was overthrown four years later.

A photograph of Empress Dowager Cixi.

erful of the eight officials, from the others, so that she could take them out one by one.

Yi Xin, Yehonala's co-conspirator, had already made preparations for a coup d'etat in Beijing. Yehonala arrived in Beijing four days earlier than Shu Shun. On the day she arrived, the imperial court raised a strong demand that Empress Yehonala should have a role in power, "behind the curtain." As had been pre-arranged, Shengbao pretended to know nothing and said, "It is obvious that you are the only one who is able to rein the government, Your Majesty cannot refuse and must take power. Otherwise, we cannot guarantee the imperial court and maintain the government." Actually the imperial court officials knew Yi Xin and Shengbao would kill them if they opposed, so no one dared to stick their neck out and argue.

The next morning, when the imperial family members and officials were as usual paying respects to the little emperor, Yehonala suddenly took out a prearranged edict written in the little emperor's name, dismissing the eight officials from their positions. She then arrested Zai Heng, Duan Hua, and others, and immediately sent people to capture Shu Shun, who was still on the way back to Beijing. Yehonala decided, along with Yi Xin and other allied officials, to behead Shu Shun whom they hated most, to order Zai Heng and Duan Hua to commit suicide, and to exile or remove the other five from their posts.

Next, Yehonala and Yi Xin arranged to have Zai Chun ascend the throne again and abolished the reign title "Qi Xiang" given by the eight officials, changing it to "Tongzhi" (Manage Together). She pretended to be modest and said, "In the Song Dynasty, there was a precedent where the empress had a role in power 'behind the curtain.' But I do not want to reign alone, so I would like to hold court with Empress Niohuru. The reign title 'Tongzhi' actually symbolizes that both of us will manage the country together."

Later, Niohuru and Yehonala were given the honorable titles "Ci'an" and "Cixi" respectively. Empress Dowager Ci'an lived in the Zhongcui Palace in the east of the Forbidden City, while Dowager Cixi resided in the Changshou Palace in the west; therefore, people also called them "Empress Dowager East" and "Empress Dowager West," respectively. Empress Dowager Ci'an was too weak to be concerned with politics. Therefore, in the ensuing over 40 years, Empress Dowager Cixi was, in reality, the sole highest ruler of the Qing Dynasty.

Empress Dowager Cixi's power "behind the curtain."

# THE SINO-JAPANESE WAR

《 The main anchor of the warship *Zhenyuan*. After Japan invaded Liugong Island, the surviving Beiyang fleet's warships were looted by Japanese troops. This main anchor of the warship *Zhenyuan* was exhibited as a trophy of the Japanese troops in Tokyo Park. Only after China's victory in the War of Resistance Against Japanese Aggression was it returned to China.

The Meiji Reformation made Japan more powerful, and it started to invade other countries. In the summer of 1894, the two Chinese warships *Jiyuan* and *Guangyi* were escorting the two trade steamboats *Gaosheng* and *Caojiang*, to take military officials and soldiers to Korea. On their way, they were attacked by the Japanese navy. The warship *Guangyi* was too small, so it retreated after it being fired upon. The warship *Jiyuan* was made of steel and powerful, but the captain Fang Boqian was a coward. As soon as he heard the firing, he fled. The soldiers on the warships *Gaosheng* and *Caojiang* bravely fought back, but unfortunately, outnumbered by their enemies, they all died in the end.

Before the Qing government could muster military reinforcements, Japan took the opportunity to launch another invasive attack. The Qing government had to declare war on Japan on August 1. This was the first Sino-Japanese War, and since this was the year of Jiawu, the war was thus also called the "War of Jiawu." The Yellow Sea Battle was one of the fiercest maritime battles during the Sino-Japanese War.

In September 1894, the Chinese Beiyang Navy commander Ding Ruchang led the Beiyang fleet on a convoy mission. On their way home, they were assaulted by a Japanese fleet at Dadonggou on the Yellow Sea; Ding Ruchang commanded his crew to immediately launch a counterattack. On the Yellow Sea, cannon-fire could be heard miles away, and smoke pervaded the air over the sea. Although the Chinese fleet had not received any advance warning, the generals and soldiers of the fleet fought back fearlessly. Ding Ruchang was severely injured, and refused to be taken below, but insisted on sitting on the deck to encourage the soldiers. Captain Deng Shichang directed his warship *Zhiyuan* to fight in front, and it was fired on the most. The ship was severely damaged, and they also ran out of ammunition. At this critical moment, Deng Shichang ordered the ship to sail in full gear and ram the enemy gunboat *Yoshino*, deciding to die with the enemy. Unfortunately, the warship *Zhiyuan* was hit by a torpedo and

Deng Shichang died with the some 200 soldiers onboard.

In this battle, due to the brave resistance of the Chinese generals and soldiers, the Japanese fleet was also badly damaged. The gunboat *Yoshino* completely lost its capabilities, the main ship *Matsushima* was destroyed, and the other three warships were seriously damaged and almost sank. The battle of the Yellow Sea confirmed the courage of the Chinese people.

However, even after the battle of the Yellow Sea, the Qing government still humiliatingly surrendered to the invaders, encouraging the Japanese invaders to launch even more fierce attacks. In February 1895, the Beiyang fleet was completely destroyed, while Ding Ruchang committed suicide for the honor of the country. Later, the Japanese enemy continued to expand their invasion. They occupied Liaodong Peninsula, the Weihai Garrison in Shandong, Penghu Islands and other places, one by one. Instead of fighting against Japan, the Qing government submitted to Japan and signed the "Treaty of Shimonoseki" with the Japanese government in April 1895, accelerating the regression of China to a semi-feudal state.

The Sino-Japanese War.

# THE HUNDRED DAYS' REFORM

⌃ Emperor Guangxu

After the Sino-Japanese War, imperialist countries expanded their invasions, and attempted to further carve up China. Some patriotic intellectuals tried to learn from the imperialist countries, restructure the feudal country's system, and reform the government, so as to strengthen the country. But under the rule of the Qing rulers, this seems unfeasible. Kang Youwei, Liang Qichao, Tan Sitong were representatives of such intellectuals.

In 1895 Kang Youwei and Liang Qichao convened over 1,300 intellectuals who were attending the imperial examination in Beijing to present a petition to Emperor Guangxu (r. 1875-1909) of the Qing Dynasty, requesting they refuse the unequal agreement with Japan, and initiate reforms. This was the famous "Joint Petition of Imperial Examination Candidates to the Emperor." Although this did not significantly change the Qing government's policy, it caused a big sensation in the country.

From the end of 1897 to early 1898, Kang Youwei petitioned Emperor Guangxu three times, stating that at this critical moment, the government should allow reformers participate in imperial court affairs, and the emperor should lead the people toward reform. Not long after, Emperor Guangxu met with Kang Youwei and conferred for two hours. In the spring of 1898, Emperor Guangxu mustered up his courage to request his power back from the Empress Dowager. He said to Yi Xin, the military minister of the time, "If the Empress Dowager still does not grant me real power, I would rather abdicate than become an emperor who witnesses the fall of the country." Empress Dowager Cixi was finally convinced by Yi Xin, and agreed to the emperor's request.

From June to September in 1898, Emperor Guangxu enacted dozens of edicts for reform, including the opening of innovative schools, the training of talented people, the translation of Western books, the popularization of a new ideology, the promo-

tion of newspapers, the expansion of avenues for free speech, the reform of government structures, the utilization of reformers, and the training of new infantry and marine forces; as well as the encouragement of private factories and enterprises. Because the year the reforms were initiated was the year of Wuxu, it was therefore also known as the "Wuxu Reforms."

Nevertheless, Emperor Guangxu could not exercise any real power, since the Qing government's power was somehow still controlled by conservatives, with Empress Dowager Cixi in the leading role. As the reforms affected their interests, the conservatives hated the reformers and strongly opposed the reforms. In September, Empress Dowager Cixi laun-ched a coup d'etat. She imprisoned Emperor Guangxu in Yingtai in Zhong-nanhai, and was present at the court to manage state affairs, and ordered the arrest of Kang Youwei, Liang Qichao, Tan Sitong and others. Kang Youwei and Liang Qichao were forced to flee to Hong Kong and Japan. By the end of September, Tan Sitong and six other reformers — called the "six honorable reformers of Wuxu" in Chinese history — were killed, and the Wuxu Reforms failed. These reforms lasted from June 11 to September 21 in 1898, a total of 103 days. It was therefore also called in history the "Hundred Days' Reform."

⌄ The joint petition of imperial examination candidates to the emperor.

# THE WUCHANG UPRISING

⌃ Eighteen-star flag (replica), 280 cm long and 165 cm wide. After the Wuchang Uprising succeeded, the Hubei military government raised this type of a flag.

In April 1911, people in Sichuan, Hubei, Hunan and Guangdong launched a road-defense movement, because the Qing government had confiscated the Sichuan-Hankou and Guangdong-Hankou railways as state-owned properties and sold the right of railway construction to a banking consortium of Britain, France, Germany and the US. The road-defense movement in Sichuan finally developed into a military rebellion. This movement soon became the catalyst for what was to be the "Wuchang Uprising."

When the movement reached its climax, the Literary Society and the Progressive Society organized by the revolutionaries in Hubei held a joint meeting in Wuchang, deciding to establish general headquarters for the revolution. They designated Jiang Yuwu, the head of the Literary Society, as commander-in-chief, and Sun Wu, in charge of the Progressive Society, as chief of staff. They contacted Huang Xing and other important figures to plan the uprising of the Hubei New Army on October 6 (Mid-Autumn Festival). But the revolution had to be postponed due to a sudden change in the state of affairs.

On the morning of October 10, Rui Cheng, the governor of Hunan and Hubei, was given a list of the revolutionaries, and he tried to have them arrested.

In such an urgent situation, Xiong Bingkun and other revolutionaries met secretly and decided to launch their revolt that very night. At 7 o'clock that evening,

Xiong Bingkun and Jin Zhaolong started the uprising of the 8th Engineering Battalion, and quickly took over the Ordnance of Chuwang Terrace; and then the other battalions rose in response. They selected Wu Zhaolin as temporary chief commander and divided into three groups to attack the governor's office. Rui Cheng became terrified out of his wits and asked people to dig a hole in the rear wall of the yamen (government office in old China); then he climbed through the hole and fled onto the warship *Chuyu*, moored earlier on the Yangtze River.

The head of the government troops, Zhang Biao, directed Qing soldiers to fight the revolutionaries in Wang-shanmen. They tried to stop the revolutionaries by utilizing the favorable terrain and advanced weapons. Xiong Bingkun organized a suicide squad of over thirty people. They crawled toward the Qing troops' front and suddenly plunged into the machine-gun position and pushed over the machine guns. Then the revolutionaries following behind rushed forward to fight their foes. Before the enemy was aware of it, the suicide squad had broken into the governor's office and burned down the hall. Zhang Biao had to retreat

⯆ The Wuchang Uprising.

孫文　天下為公　逢伯先生屬

Sun Yat-sen's calligraphy *The Country for All.*

when he saw the office on fire.

After one night of fierce battle, the revolutionaries took over the government office and all of Wuchang City. On the morning of October 11, the revolutionary troops' flag was raised on the Wuchang city wall. The revolutionaries had won! Li Yuanhong, the deputy captain of the New Army, was selected to be governor-general of the newly established military government, while Tang Hualong became the minister of the civil administration. They declared a nationwide uprising. This uprising, originating in Wuchang, was hence named the "Wuchang Uprising."

The Wuchang Uprising ignited a nationwide revolutionary surge and contributed to the establishment of a democratic republic — the Republic of China — in Nanjing on 1 January 1912, with Sun Yat-sen assuming the presidency. In February 1912, the Qing emperor abdicated, symbolizing the end of the 268-year Qing Dynasty and over 2,000 years of absolute monarchy. Later, China went through the War of Resistance Against Japanese Aggression and the War of Liberation. Ultimately, the Chinese people triumphed in the New Democratic Revolution, and following the lead of the Chinese Communist Party, the People's Republic of China was founded. The founding of the People's Republic of China announced the rebirth of the Chinese nation.

≫ A statue of Sun Yat-sen.

⊙ The Founding of the Republic of China

When the Wuchang Uprising was supported by the whole country, Sun Yat-sen returned from overseas to Shanghai and the revolutionary party began preparing to establish a temporary government of republic. On December 20, 1911, the conference of representatives from 17 provinces was held in Nanjing, which decided to set up the provisional government and chose Sun Yat-sen the first president. At the inauguration at 11 p.m. of that day, Sun Yat-sen swore in to be the president and issued at the same time the "Announcement of the Provisional President," and the "Letter to All Compatriots." The country was called "Republic of China," and began using the Gregorian calendar. Sun Yat-sen set the day of January 1, 1912 as the beginning of the Republic of China and sent a circular telegram to all provinces on January 2, 1912, asking them to use the new calendar.

# A Brief Chronology of Chinese History

| | | | |
|---|---|---|---|
| Xia Dynasty | | | 2070 BC — 1600 BC |
| Shang Dynasty | | | 1600 BC — 1046 BC |
| Western Zhou Dynasty | | | 1046 BC — 771 BC |
| Eastern Zhou Dynasty | | Spring and Autumn Period | 770 BC — 476 BC |
| | | Warring States Period | 475 BC — 221 BC (Zhou fell in 256 BC) |
| Qin Dynasty | | | 221 BC — 206 BC |
| Han Dynasty | | Western Han | 206 BC — 25 AD |
| | | Eastern Han | 25 — 220 |
| Three Kingdoms | | Wei | 220 — 265 |
| | | Shu | 221 — 263 |
| | | Wu | 222 — 280 |
| Jin Dynasty | | Western Jin | 265 — 317 |
| | | Eastern Jin | 317 — 420 |
| Northern and Southern Dynasties | Southern Dynasties | Song | 420 — 479 |
| | | Qi | 479 — 502 |
| | | Liang | 502 — 557 |
| | | Chen | 557 — 589 |
| | Northern Dynasties | Northern Wei | 386 — 534 |
| | | Eastern Wei | 534 — 550 |
| | | Northern Qi | 550 — 577 |
| | | Western Wei | 535 — 556 |
| | | Northern Zhou | 557 — 581 |
| Sui Dynasty | | | 581 — 618 |
| Tang Dynasty | | | 618 — 907 |
| Five Dynasties | | Later Liang | 907 — 923 |
| | | Later Tang | 923 — 936 |
| | | Later Jin | 936 — 947 |
| | | Later Han | 947 — 950 |
| | | Later Zhou | 951 — 960 |
| Song Dynasty | | Northern Song | 960 — 1127 |
| | | Southern Song | 1127 — 1279 |
| Liao | | | 907 — 1125 |
| Jin | | | 1115 — 1234 |
| Yuan Dynasty | | | 1271 — 1368 |
| Ming Dynasty | | | 1368 — 1644 |
| Qing Dynasty | | | 1644 — 1911 |

**图书在版编目（CIP）数据**

中华上下五千年／张延图主编.
－北京：外文出版社，2006
（中华典籍图文系列）
ISBN 978-7-119-04636-5

I. 中...    II. 张...    III. 中国－通史－普及读物－英文    IV. K209

中国版本图书馆 CIP 数据核字（2006）第 118414 号


策　　划　邵　东
英文翻译　闫威　黄少杰　许效礼　李洋　周晓刚　王琴　欧阳伟萍　冯鑫
英文审定　May Yee　王明杰
责任编辑　蔡莉莉　樊文龙
绘　　图　刘安利
装帧设计　夏　鹏　等
版式制作　北京京鲁创业科贸有限公司
印刷监制　冯　浩

（本书图片由北京日知图书、中国文物交流中心等提供）

中 华 上 下 五 千 年

张延图　主编

*

© 外文出版社

外文出版社出版

（中国北京百万庄大街 24 号）

邮政编码　100037

外文出版社网址：http://www.flp.com.cn

外文印刷厂印刷

中国国际图书贸易总公司发行

（中国北京车公庄西路 35 号）

北京邮政信箱第 399 号　邮政编码 100044

2007 年(大 16 开)第 1 版

2011 年第 1 版第 4 次印刷

（英）

ISBN 978-7-119-04636-5

15000(精)

85-E-634S